HYMN NOTES

For

CHURCH BULLETINS

By

Austin C. Lovelace
Fellow, Hymn Society of America

G.I.A. Publications, Inc.
Chicago

ISBN: 0-941050-09-2

FOREWORD

I will sing with the spirit, and I will sing with the understanding, also.
1 Corinthians 14: 15
King James Version

This often quoted passage from Paul's letter to the Corinthians is the purpose of this valuable worship aid. The worshiper needs to know that hymns grow out of individual and corporate experiences. The great hymn writers have experienced the faith and are eager to pass it on. It is the duty of the worship leader, minister and musician, to assist the worshiper in understanding.

The printed media in a congregation, newsletters and worship bulletins, should contain information about how and why we worship. The short hymn paragraphs contained in this book provide information which will assist the worshiper in understanding the faith through hymns.

Austin Lovelace has spent his life singing the faith through hymns. Because of his devotion to the faith, his knowledge of hymnology, and his concern for the worshiper, he agreed to write this volume of HYMN NOTES, as requested by The Hymn Society of America.

Now it is the responsibility of all ministers and musicians to put these HYMN NOTES to work. With this outstanding resource worshipers can accept the challenge of Paul to sing with spirit and understanding.

W. Thomas Smith
Executive Director
The Hymn Society of America

PREFACE

These Hymn Notes are specifically designed for publication in church bulletins, and purchase of this book carries with it permission to reprint any or all of them in worship bulletins, church papers and educational materials. With this purpose in mind, the notes have been kept brief, including only that information which seemed most likely to be of help and interest to the congregation.

The most difficult task has been to decide from the wealth of material available as to what would be most meaingful. Behind every hymn there is a multitude of facts and stories available in hymn studies and handbooks to hymnals, but some information would be of interest only to serious students of hymnology, ecclesiology, biography, theology and poetry. Some of the questions which have been addressed are: WHO, WHEN, WHAT, WHY, HOW. "Who" deals with the fascinating people who wrote hymns. "When" often explains factors that place a hymn in its historical context. "What" deals with the actual content of hymns, especially when they are based on scriptural passages. "Why" helps to explain the reasons behind the writing, for all hymns represent some spiritual insight or experience which the poet felt compelled to put on paper to share with others. "How" is concerned with structural and poetic devices — a subject of much more importance than most people realize. (For a study of this in depth I refer the reader to my small volume, "The Anatomy of Hymnody", published by G.I.A. Publications, Inc.).

For each hymn the author, with dates, and translator(s), with dates, is given first. The "Source" gives the first publication of the hymn if known. This may be omitted from the bulletin if it is felt the information would not be of sufficient interest. This is followed by several sentences of information, which may be shortened if you wish or may be expanded with other details from information available in handbooks.

It is impossible to provide notes for every hymn in every hymnal, but over 400 hymns have been chosen which seem to be most commonly found in major American hymnals. If the hymn is not here, seek out material (a bibliography of available sources is appended to this volume) and write your own notes.

Hymn singing is one of the most basic responses in worship, and the first job of the ministry of music should be the improvement of hymn singing by educating the congregation in the reasons for singing and in giving them information about hymns. The more informed the congregation, the better the singing, the deeper the worship experience, and the wider the response to choral participation in specialized choirs. But the congregation is always the first choir.

The writing of this book has involved research in many volumes, but I wish to pay tribute to a special group of books which has been most helpful. Frank Colquhoun's "A Hymn Companion: Insight into 300 Christian Hymns" is similar in purpose and is written by a minister who is most knowledgeable about hymns and theology. Erik Routley's "An English-Speaking Hymnal Guide" is a gold mine of historical detail by this century's most outstanding hymnologist. Marilyn Stulken's "Hymnal Companion to the Lutheran Book of Worship" is most scholarly and helpful. The "Companion to the Hymnal" (Methodist Hymnal, 1964) by Fred D. Gealy, Austin C. Lovelace, and Carlton R. Young covers a large majority of hymns taken from the Ecumenical Hymn List. Albert C. Ronander and Ethel K. Poerter's thorough work in "Guide to the Pilgrim Hymnal" has been helpful for many hymns not found elsewhere. And William J. Reynolds' "Hymns of Our Faith: A Handbook for the Baptist Hymnal" and Donald P. Hustad's "Dictionary-Handbook to Hymns for the Living Church" have provided information on many of the gospel songs. In addition handbooks for various denominational hymnals have been consulted for specific hymns not generally found elsewhere.

I can do no better than to quote Frank Colquhoun in his Preface to "A Hymn Companion", for this statement of purpose is the same as mine: "My purpose has been to provide a popular work of reference giving information about a representative selection of hymns now in general use. It is written not for the experts, who already have their own books on the subject, but for hymn-lovers in general; for churchgoers and non-churchgoers alike; for clergy, ministers, teachers, choristers and others who whose work involves the use of hymns....My hope is that this may enable those who sing hymns to appreciate them better and to sing them with more understanding."

A charge to keep, I have
Charles Wesley, 1707-1788
Source: *Short Hymns on Select Passages of Holy Scripture,* 1762
   Wesley published two volumes containing 2,030 hymns based upon scripture from Genesis to Revelation. Sixteen were inspired by the book of Leviticus! This hymn can be summarised by Wesley's heading, "Keep the charge of the Lord, that ye die not." (Leviticus 8:35)

A hymn of glory let us sing!
The Venerable Bede, 673-735
Source: Eleventh century manuscript, British Museum
   This is a hymn of pure praise! The events of the ascension of Christ are dramatically related to the Christian's hope for eternal life. The 1200 year old Latin text by the monk Bede has thrived through many translations into many languages.

A mighty fortress is our God
Martin Luther, 1483-1546
Source: *Geistliche Lieder,* Wittenberg, 1529
   This "Battle Hymn of the Reformation" is based on portions of Psalm 46, scripture being the inspiration for a number of Luther hymns. The final stanza is Luther's vow, and ours, to cling to God's Word and Truth in spite of the stresses of this life.

A stable lamp is lighted
Richard P. Wilbur, b. 1921
Source: *Advice to a Prophet and Other Poems,* 1961
   Jesus states in Luke 19:40 that if his disciples were forced to refrain from praise "the very stones would cry out." Wilbur's use of "every stone shall cry" is an effective unifying device in the poem which moves from the birth of Christ through passion and resurrection back to Mary's song (the Magnificat.) Wilbur is one of America's leading poets.

Abide with me
Henry F. Lyte, 1793-1847
Source: Leaflet with tune by author, 1847
   Although the hymn is often considered an evening hymn, it is really about the eventide of life. The author suffered from severe illness most of his life, and yet this hymn faces death with strength and hope. This positive hymn continues to be an inspiration to Christians throughout the English-speaking world.

Ah, Holy Jesus, how hast Thou offended
Johann Heermann, 1585-1647
Trans. Robert S. Bridges, 1844-1930
Source: Heermann, *Devoti Musica Cordis,* 1630 based on
   Meditations VII, attr. to Augustine

The author's many tribulations (severely ill as a child, eye troubles, his wife's death, losing all possessions in the Thirty Years' War, the pestilence of 1631, and forced retirement from the ministry by throat trouble) found a sympathetic note in the medieval meditation on the underserved sufferings of Christ. Understanding the sufferings of others, we receive strength from this hymn.

Alas! and did my Savior bleed
Isaac Watts, 1674-1748
Source: *Hymns and Spiritual Songs,* 1707

As a poet writing about the sufferings of Christ, Watts stands supreme. This hymn, entitled "Godly Sorrow arising from the Sufferings of Christ," is a companion to "When I survey the wondrous cross," which is probably the greatest hymn ever written. Stanza one ended "For such a worm as I," but is now always changed to "sinners such as I." Humankind with all its sins is certainly above the status of a worm! The phrase "God, the mighty maker died" is a powerful figurative paradox. How amazing to say that God the creator should die for man the creature. Such love demands all that we have and are.

All beautiful the march of days
Frances W. Wile, 1878-1939
Source: *Unity Hymns and Carols,* 1911

Lacking a good hymn about winter, Dr. William Channing Gannett, minister of First Unitarian Church in Rochester, NY, asked Mrs. Wile to write one. The two years spent in writing and polishing resulted in a jewel which links the snowy landscapes with the hearth of home and the handiwork of the Creator. It is based on Job 38:22: "Hast thou entered into the treasures of the snow?"

All creatures of our God and King
Francis of Assisi, c. 1182-1226
Trans. William H. Draper, 1855-1933
Source: *Hymns of the Spirit,* 1926

The life of the founder of the Franciscan monastic order is most astounding. Born to wealth, he forsook all for a life of asceticism, mysticism and charitable works with the sick and downtrodden. It is said that he even preached to the birds and they listened! An early environmentalist, his "Canticle of the Sun" was the first genuine religious poem in the Italian language. St. Francis saw all of nature and everything — including death — as praising God.

All glory be to God on high
Nikolaus Decius, 1490-1541
Trans. Catherine Winkworth, 1827-1878
Source: Rostock *Gesang Buch,* 1525
Decius, a Catholic monk who became an evangelical preacher under the influence of Martin Luther, was, like many ministers of the period, equally effective as a poet and musician. (He wrote the tune as well as the words.) Based on the angel's Christmas hymn, *Gloria in excelsis,* it comes to life in the brilliant translation of Catherine Winkworth.

All glory, laud and honor
Theodulph of Orleans, c. 750-821
Trans. John Mason Neale, 1818-1866
Source: *Medieval Hymns,* 1851
Bishop Theodulph was imprisoned in 818 for conspiring against King Louis the Pious. This hymn was probably written while in prison, originally in 78 lines which was shortened and translated from the Latin by Neale. It has become the traditional Palm Sunday processional hymn throughout the church.

All hail the power of Jesus' name
Edward Perronet, 1726-1792. Alt. by John Rippon, 1751-1836
Source: *Gospel Magazine,* 1780
Written by a friend and advisor of the Wesleys who later became a Congregational minister, the text has had many alterations. Rippon, famous for including "How firm a foundation" in his 1791 hymnal, added two new stanzas and extensively rewrote the others. Its extravagant praise and "crown Him" chorus become exuberant when sung to CORONATION, DIADEM, or MILES LANE — all equally popular tunes.

All my heart this night rejoices
Paul Gerhardt, 1607-1676
Trans. Catherine Winkworth, 1827-1878
Source: *Praxis Pietatis Melica,* 1653
Gerhardt's personal and warm text invites us to share in the excitement and joy of that first Christmas eve. Crüger's tune, while rhythmically varied, is easy to sing because of its use of short sequences which match the unusual meter of the poetry.

All my hope on God is founded
Joachim Neander, 1650-1680. Trans. Robert Bridges, 1844-1930
Source: *Joachimi Neandri Glaub-und Liebesübung,* 1680
   Based on I Timothy 6:17, "God who richly furnishes us with everything to enjoy," the words were intended to be sung as a "grace
after meat." The famous "Neanderthal man" was found in a cave
on the Rhine river where the author once lived, and was so named
to honor him — a most unusual recognition for a hymn writer!

All people that on earth do dwell
William Kethe, d. 1594
Source: *Anglo-Genevan Psalter,* 1561
   Having been exiled from Scotland during a religious persecution,
the author was influenced by the style of psalm paraphrases sung
in Geneva. He had in mind the famous "Doxology" tune (OLD
HUNDREDTH) by Bourgeois, music editor for the Genevan Psalter
of 1551. It is the oldest English metrical psalm in use today.

All praise to Thee, for Thou, O King divine
F. Bland Tucker, 1895-1985
Source: *Hymnal,* 1940
   Tucker's paraphrase of Philippians 2:5-11 is one of the finest
versions of the call to have the "mind of Christ," urging us to share
his humility. The author served on the committees for both Episcopal hymnals of 1940 and 1982, where his first rate Greek translations first appeared.

All praise to Thee, my God, this night
Thomas Ken, 1637-1710
Source: *Manual of Prayers,* 1695
   Imagine living at a time when only the psalms could be sung in
church — no hymns. Bishop Ken wrote three hymns (Morning, Evening, Midnight) for the young scholars at Winchester College "to sing
in your Chamber devoutly." The evening hymn owes much of its
popularity to the tune by Thomas Tallis which can be sung as a round
in two, four, or even eight parts.

All the way my Savior leads me
Fanny J. Crosby, 1820-1915
Source: *Brightest and Best,* 1875
   The author, blind at six weeks of age, began writing verse at eight
years, and her total number of religious verse has been estimated
between 8,500 and 15,000. She was commissioned by all the famous
tune writers of her day to write texts for them, as many as three a

week, and many under pseudonyms. This text was written as she meditated on the goodness of God after receiving an unexpected good fortune.

All things bright and beautiful
Cecil Frances Alexander, 1818-1895
Source: *Hymns for Little Children,* 1848
   The wife of an Anglican bishop, Mrs. Alexander wrote nearly 400 hymns, the most famous of which are those written to teach children the meaning of various parts of the Apostles' Creed. The simple yet picturesque words help to describe the phrase "Maker of heaven and earth," which is based on Genesis 1:31: "And God saw everything that he had made, and behold, it was very good."

All who love and serve your city
Erik Routley, 1917-1982
Source: *Dunblane Praises II,* 1967
   Until recently few hymns were written about city life. Reflecting on the Watts' riots in Los Angeles, Routley combined Jesus' concern for doing God's work (John 9:40) with the prophetic view of the City of God found in Ezekiel 48:35: "And the name of the city henceforth shall be, The Lord is there." The author was undoubtedly one of the most brilliant hymnologists and theologians of this century. This was his first hymn, written in 1966.

Alleluia, sing to Jesus
William C. Dix, 1837-1898
Source: *Altar Songs,* 1867
   One usually does not expect an insurance agent to write hymns, but Dix turned to the field of letters and wrote this text as a new Communion hymn for the Church of England. However, the "communion" stanza is usually omitted, making the text more generally useful for praise, adoration or Ascension.

Alleluia, song of gladness (sweetness)
Latin, 11th century. Trans. John Mason Neale, 1818-1866
Source: *Hymnal Noted,* 1852
   The word "Alleluia" (Praise ye the Lord/Jehovah) is the epitome of praise in church language, but during Lent Medieval custom (still preserved in many churches today) forbade the use of the word during Lent. So this hymn was intended as a "farewell to Alleuia," to be sung the Sunday or the day before Ash Wednesday. As late as the 15th century there was a ceremony of burying "Alleluia" in a coffin on Ash Wednesday, with the word to be revived and sung again

on Easter day.

Alone Thou goest forth to die
Peter Abelard, 1079-1142. Trans. F. Bland Tucker, 1895-1985
Source: *Hymnarium Paraclitensis,* c. 1135
   The story of Abelard and Heloise would make a good soap opera. The famous lecturer at the Cathedral School of Notre Dame falls in love with the daughter of Canon Fulbert who vows revenge and hounds Abelard to his death. The two become monk and nun, and Abelard writes a complete cycle of hymns for her based on the various services sung during the church year. This text is for Good Friday.

Amazing grace! how sweet the sound
John Newton, 1725-1807
Source: *Olney Hymns,* 1779
   Based on King David's review of his kingdom before the Lord (I Chronicles 17:16-17) and entitled "faith's review and expectations," the text is a personal testimomy of a man whose early life on a slave ship was turned around by an "amazing grace" that "saved a wretch like me." His experience has been duplicated by a host of singers who have been saved by the grace of God, and find comfort in singing this hymn.

And can it be that I should gain
Charles Wesley, 1707-1788
Source: *Psalms and Hymns,* 1738
   This is an historic text, written in London, May 1738, two days after Charles' conversion experience. Two days later, and the day after John Wesley's Aldersgate experience, they sang it together on May 25. Based on the story of Paul and Silas singing and praying in prison at midnight (Acts 16:25), it is a profound poetic expression of an intense spiritual experience.

And have the bright immensities
Howard Chandler Robbins, 1876-1952
Source: *Living Church,* 1931
   Few hymns begin successfully with the word "And," but Robbins, an Episcopal clergyman and seminary professor has tackled an even more difficult assignment: to make sense out of the Ascension for today's church. "Bright immensities" is contrasted with "altar candle," and stanza one, a complete question, is answered in the second by suggesting that Christ "ascended" into the church, and that whenever we gather to worship and to celebrate the sacrament He is present in our midst.

And now, O Father, mindful of the love
William Bright, 1824-1901
Source: *The Monthly Packet,* 1873
The author, a brilliant scholar who became Canon at Christ Church, Oxford, at the age of forty-four, wrote many prayers and collects for the 1928 *Book of Common Prayer* for England. His communion hymn recognizes the "one, true, pure, immortal sacrifice" of Christ for us, and prays that we may be forgiven our sins, allowed to partake of the feast and to go forth in service to others.

Angels, from the realms of glory
James Montgomery, 1771-1854
Source: *Sheffield Iris,* 1816
Raised in a Moravian family of missionary parents, Montgomery was attracted by the Wesleys' social concerns and later, when he became editor of the *Sheffield Iris,* he championed many unpopular causes, being twice imprisoned for reporting news unfavorable to the government. The hymn is a call for all (angels, shepherds, wise men, saints and us) to come and worship the new-born King as told in the Christmas stories of Luke 2 and Matthew 2.

Angels we have heard on high
Traditional French Carol
Source: *Nouveau recueil de cantiques,* 1855
The French original probably comes from the 1700's although it was first published a century later. As with all carols, the popular folk melody carries equal weight and importance for the success of the work, and half the fun is singing the "Gloria" refrain.

As men of old their first fruits brought
Frank von Christierson, b. 1900
Source: Hymn Society of America, 1961
The author, a Presbyterian minister, submitted this text to the Department of Stewardship and Benevolence of the National Council of Churches of Christ in the U.S.A. and the Hymn Society of America, who were seeking new hymns on "Stewardship." Ten hymns were chosen, and this has outpaced all others in popularity. We must be good stewards today of all that God has given us, just as the farmers of old brought their first and best fruits to God, the Giver of all good.

As pants the hart for cooling stream
Psalm 42, *New Version.* Tate and Brady, 1696
Source: *New Version of the Psalms* of David, 1696

Tate and Brady are famous for their "new version" of the Psalms, which replaced the "old version" of Sternhold and Hopkins, 1562. This is one of three psalm versions to survive. It is based on Psalm 42, and was altered by Henry F. Lyte, Anglican clergyman.

As with gladness men of old
William C. Dix, 1837-1898
Source: *Hymns of Love and Joy*, 1861
(*Hymns Ancient and Modern*, 1859)
First published in a trial edition of the incredibly successful *Hymns Ancient and Modern* (1859) (over 100 million copies have been sold in various editions), this has become one of the most famous hymns for Epiphany. It is based on the Gospel lesson from Matthew 2:1-12 for Epiphany Day and tells of the visit of the Magi.

At even when the sun was set
Henry Twells, 1823-1900
Source: *Hymns Ancient and Modern*, 1868
In Mark 1:32-34 we are told that at sundown those who were sick or possessed with demons were brought to Jesus to heal. Twells originally wrote "ere the sun was set," but since according to Jewish law no one would have dared to bring anyone to Jesus for healing until after sunset, the first line has been altered. The themes of evening and of healing are combined.

At the cross her station keeping
(Also: "Near the cross her vigil keeping")
Jacopone da Todi, 1230-1306
Trans. Anthony G. Petti, 1932-1985
Source: *Roman Missal*, 1727
Although the text has been attributed to Pope Gregory the Great, Bernard of Clairvaux, Bonaventura, Pope John XXII, Pope Gregory XI, and Pope Innocent III, it is probably by the lawyer-turned-Franciscan priest. Intended for devotional usage, it was widely sung by Flagellants in the 14th century. Its deep piety and intense devotional quality have led many famous composers to make extended choral settings of many movements.

At the Lamb's high feast
Anon. Latin, before 1000. Trans. Robert Campbell, 1814-1868
Source: Trans. *St. Andrew's Hymnal*, 1850
Especially suitable for the Easter Vigil, this hymn contains an unusual richness of medieval Easter imagery including white robes of baptism, the Exodus story of deliverance through the Red Sea,

and the Altar as symbolic of the Cross. On Easter Even the catechumens, dressed in white, were baptized, confirmed, and went to their first communion on Easter morning. A popular hymn, it was widely sung in Anglican, Roman, Mozarabic, and Ambrosian rites.

At the name of Jesus
Caroline M. Noel, 1817-1877
Source: *The Name of Jesus, and Other Poems for the Sick and Lonely,* 1870
Some hymns are for praise, some for prayer, some for teaching and instructing, and some narratives to tell a story. This hymn is based on Philippians 2:5-11, and in many ways combines all three. It was written as a processional hymn for Ascension Day.

Awake, awake to love and work
G. A. Studdert-Kennedy, 1883-1929
Source: *Sorrows of God and other Poems,* 1921
The author was a famous chaplain known as "Woodbine Willie" in World War I. Written to be sung "At a Harvest Festival," the hymn is a call to rise each morning with our souls ablaze, ready to give ourselves to God's service as freely as He has given us this glorious fresh new world each day. Note there is a comma at the end of stanza two; so the thought must be carried over to the last stanza.

Awake, my soul, and with the sun
Thomas Ken, 1637-1710
Source: *Manual of Prayers,* 1695
Bishop Ken's hymns were written for the boys at Winchester College to sing privately in the morning and evening. Few texts are finer for morning devotions and preparation for the day. The stanza beginning "Direct, control, suggest this day" is especially appropriate. Like the evening hymn, "All praise to Thee, my God this night," it ends with a stanza which we call the "Doxology" — "Praise God, from whom all blesings flow."

Awake, my soul, stretch every nerve
Philip Doddridge, 1702-1751
Source: *Hymns,* published posthumously 1755
Because the author, an English Dissenting minister, wrote all of his hymns to follow and sum up his sermons, his works are strongly biblically based. In this hymn, in addition to "Pressing onward in the Christian race" (Philippians 3:12-14) there are references to Corinthians 9:24; Hebrews 12:1; II Timothy 4:8; and Revelation 4:10. Read over these references before you sing the hymn so that you

may find deeper meanings in the hymn.

Awake, O sleeper, arise from death
F. Bland Tucker, 1895-1983
Source: Anthem setting by David N. Johnson, Augsburg
Publishing House, 1980

This hymn is a concise poetic·summation of chapters 3, 4 and 5 of Ephesians, with the opening line taken from Ephesians 5:14, which may have been part of a baptism hymn. Stanzas 2 and 3 are credal in nature, with emphasis on our oneness in Christ. Stanzas 4 and 5 are a call for us to follow Christ in our daily living. The author was a scholarly Episcopal priest famous for his superb translations of Greek and Latin hymnody as well as for several original hymns, all scripturally inspired.

Away in a manager
Anon. 19th century
Source: *Little Children's Book for Schools and Family*, 1885

Picking up the text from a Philadelphia book, J.R. Murray included it in *Dainty Songs for Little Lads and Lassies* with his tune, but with the false information that the text was by Martin Luther. While Luther did write a long Christmas hymn ("From heaven above to earth I come") for his children, this text is by the famous "Anonymous." The simple story is easily learned and long remembered and loved.

Be known to us in breaking bread
James Montgomery, 1771-1854
Source: *Christian Psalmist*, 1825

Many of our favorite hymns were originally written as table graces. The Moravian poet-newspaper editor based his hymn on the Emmaus story in Luke 24:30-31 in which Christ was recognized in the breaking of bread. It is one of our finest post-Easter communion hymns because of its Scriptural basis and its short and direct prayer that Christ will sup with us as He did with the people at Emmaus.

Be Thou my vision
Irish Anon. Trans. Mary E. Byrne, 1880-1931. Versed by
Eleanor H. Hull, 1860-1935
Source: *Erin*, vol. 2, 1905

In a time when the "now" seems to be most important, it is help-ful to sing hymns which remind us that throughout the ages the church has produced great ideas which are still valid and useful today. Written around the 8th century, the text has become popular since 1927 when it was wedded to the memorable Irish tune SLANE with its ABCD form (each line of music is different).

Beautiful Savior (See: "Fairest Lord Jesus")

Before Jehovah's awful throne
Isaac Watts, 1674-1748. Alt. John Wesley, 1703-1791
Source: *The Psalms of David Imitated,* 1719
   The word "awful" (awefull) has been a stumbling block for many, for the original meaning of "awe" has been lost. It is interesting to compare Watts' version of Psalm 100 (as altered by John Wesley) with the more popular "All people that on earth do dwell" by William Kethe. Watts is more somber and severe, presenting God as sovereign ruler. Yet stanza three invites us to crowd His gates and courts singing praise.

Beneath the cross of Jesus
Elizabeth C. Clephane, 1830-1869
Source: *The Family Treasury,* pub. posthumously 1872
   The author, who spent most of her life in Melrose, the home of Sir Walter Scott, wrote this personal statement shortly before her death about her feelings while meditating on the meaning of the cross. She was nicknamed "Sunbeam" because of her philanthropic work among the poor. Victorian in style and language, it still holds a popular place in Holy Week services.

Blessed Jesus at Thy word
Tobias Clausnitzer, 1619-1684
Trans. Catherine Winkworth, 1827-1878
Source: *Altdorffisches Gesangbüchlein,* 1663
   Do you look forward to hearing the Scriptures read in a service? The author wrote his hymn to indicate the reason to gather for worship is to hear the Word of God, and this text was designed to be sung before the sermon. Originally there were seven stanzas (including one about the Nicene Creed), but usually only three are sung, and sometimes only one.

Blessing and honor and glory and power
Horatius Bonar, 1808-1889
Source: *Hymns of Faith and Hope, III,* 1866
   Bonar, a dedicated and successful minister in the Church of Scotland, wrote voluminously — nearly one book a year — including some 600 hymns. By piling up words (blessing-honor-glory-power; the kingdom, the crown, and the throne; the robe and the harp and the psalm) he imitates successfully a poetic device used by Isaac Watts.

Its ringing praise echoes the high flown language of many passages from Revelation.

Blest are the pure in heart
John Keble, 1792-1866
Source: *The Christian Year*, 1827

Keble's most famous work is his collection of hymns written for all of the various seasons of the church year. This text is based on Matthew 5:3 (the Beatitudes) and originally had seventeen stanzas. Reduced to four stanzas by most hymnal editors, it is still a powerful call to us to be pure in heart.

Blest be the tie that binds
John Fawcett, 1740-1817
Source: *Hymns*, 1782

Fawcett, an English Baptist minister in Yorkshire, received a call to a bigger and more prestigious church in London. After preaching his farewell sermon and loading his luggage on the wagons, he decided that he would prefer to stay with his fellowship in the smaller church. In its first publication in 1782 it was titled "Brotherly Love." It is widely used as a closing prayer at many church gatherings.

Book of books, our people's strength
Percy Dearmer, 1867-1936
Source: *Songs of Praise*, 1925

How did we get the Bible as we know it? Dearmer's hymn is a reminder that many people have had a hand in completing scrolls, translating, struggling over ancient manuscripts — but all telling the story of the Word made flesh. So we sing this text to God who the inspiration of the Bible.

Bread of heaven, on Thee we feed
Josiah Conder, 1789-1855
Source: *Star in the East*, 1824

People were startled when Jesus said "I am the living bread...and the bread which I shall give for the life of the world is my flesh" and "I am the true vine" (John 6:51-54 and John 15:1). Conder's hymn is based on these two passages and was entitled "For the Eucharist," the feast of gladness. The author, a leading Congregational layman, was the editor of the first official hymn for the Congregational Union of England and Wales.

Bread of the world, in mercy broken
Reginald Heber, 1783-1826

Source: *Hymns Written and Adapted to the Weekly Service of the Church Year,* 1827

In the 19th century, the new romantic style allowed poetic imagination to become more important than merely correct dogma. When sung devotionally "Before the Sacrament" as Heber intended it, the hymn invites us to confess our sins and to accept the grace of God as our souls are fed.

Break forth, O beauteous, heavenly light
Johann Rist, 1607-1667
Source: *Himmlische Lieder,* 1641
Trans. John Troutbeck, 1833-1889

J.S. Bach included hymns in his cantatas and oratorios, and we owe the inclusion of this single stanza to its use in his "Christmas Oratorio." The author was both a Lutheran pastor and physician who lost all his personal property during the Thirty Years' War. Author of around 680 hymns, he was named Poet Laureate in 1645 by Emperor Ferdinand III.

Break Thou the bread of life
Mary Artemesia Lathbury, 1841-1913
Source: *Chautauqua Carols,* 1878

It is all too easy to be content with merely reading the Bible through, but Mary Lathbury asks for more — that we seek the Lord beyond the sacred page and find the truth which is God. Daughter of a Methodist minister, the author wrote the hymn for use at Chautauqua in New York state in groups devoted to Bible study. Although it mentions bread, it is not a Communion hymn.

Breathe on me, breath of God
Edwin Hatch, 1835-1889
Source: Leaflet, "Between Doubt and Prayer," 1878

Since in both Hebrew and Greek the word for "spirit" is "wind" or "air," the author calls the Spirit of God the Breath of God. Therefore the heart of the hymn is in the life of the Spirit, ending with "the perfect life of eternity," untouched by death. The author was a great scholar, yet a humble man whose hymn reflects a personal relationship with the Holy Spirit rather than an historical or theological one.

Brightest and best of the sons of the morning
Reginald Heber, 1783-1826
Source: *Christian Observer,* November 1811

Heber's interest in the church led him to write a series of hymns for the Christian year, this being designated "Epiphany" and meant to be sung between the creed and sermon. While it uses natural imagery, its concern is to make clear what is acceptable worship to God as stated in Psalm 51:17: "The sacrifices of God are a broken spirit: a broken and a contrite heart, O God, Thou wilt not despise."

Built on the (a) rock the church shall (doth) stand
Nicolai Grundtvig, 1783-1872. Trans. Carl Doving, 1867-1937
Source: *Sang-Värk til den Danske Kirke,* 1837
The Danish author was a contemporary of Sören Kierkegaard (with whom he disagreed theologically) and was more famous and influential during his lifetime. Based on the story of Christ calling Peter the rock on which the church is built, the hymn is a reminder that we are the building blocks, the living stones which comprise the church in which God deigns to dwell. It is our duty to make that temple holy and to lead our children to God's Kingdom.

Chief of sinners though I be
William McComb, 1793-c. 1870
Source: *The Poetical Works of William McComb,* 1864
The author was a bookseller and publisher in Belfast, Ireland. His hymn is a personal statement of thanks to Christ for his acts in providing the road to salvation and support to avoid temptation to sin. Its message is simple and straightforward, and is well carried by Redhead's famous tune GETHSEMANE.

Children of the heavenly Father
Caroline V. Sandell Berg, 1832-1903
Trans. Ernest W. Olson, 1870-1958
Source: *Fourteen Hymns,* 1858
The author, known as the Fanny Crosby of Sweden, began writing hymns as a result of the drowning of her father in 1858. She wrote around 1650 pieces in a warm, personal, evangelical, revival style. This is her most famous work in American hymnals and owes much of its popularity to the simple, child-like folk melody to which it is set.

Christ is alive! Let Christians sing
Brian A. Wren, b. 1936
Source: *New Church Praise,* 1975
Wren, a minister in the United Reformed Church of England and Wales, is one of the shining lights in contemporary English hymnody. The cross is empty, and Christ is alive here and now — not tied down to 2000 years ago in Palestine. This is one of the finest

new hymns about the meaning of the Resurrection for today.

Christ is arisen
Anon. German c. 1100
Source: Several 12th century sources
  This is the oldest of five sequences still in use in the Roman Catholic church, and was the basis for the beginnings of liturgical drama. The text and tune were favorites of Martin Luther. Of the many translations, the most famous is by Miles Coverdale (1488-1569). Don't let the austerity of the modal melody frighten you. As Luther said, "After a time one tires of singing all other hymns, but 'Christ is erstanden' one can always sing again."

Christ is made the sure foundation
Latin, c. 7th century. Trans. John Mason Neale, 1818-1866
Source: *Hymnal Noted*, 1852
  The ancient Latin hymn from the 7th century about blessed Jerusalem is based on St. Paul's description of the church in Ephesians 2:20, 21: "build upon the foundation of the apostles and prophets, Christ Jesus himself being the chief corner-stone, in whom the whole structure is joined together and grows into a holy temple in the Lord." As "living stones" we are joined together to form a "spiritual house" with Christ as the foundation of all.

Christ is the King! O friends rejoice
George Kennedy Allen Bell, 1883-1958
Source: *Songs of Praise*, 1931
  A scarcity of hymns suitable for the Feast of St. Simon and St. Jude (October 28) led the famous hymnal editor Percy Dearmer to request that the author, then dean of Canterbury, to write this hymn. It is a call for an ecumenical church, when at last all believers and denominations will be one and "God's will on earth be done."

Christ is the world's true light
George W. Briggs, 1875-1959
Source: *Songs of Praise*, 1931
  Briggs, an Anglican clergyman, has been called by Erik Routley "unquestionably the leading hymn writer of his generation in Britain." The author described this as "essentially a missionary hymn" and its missionary character and cosmic outlook are evident. Christ is the world's light, its peace uniting nations and peoples, and its hope for a kingdom of righteousness. Each of us should make the closing prayer our own: "Come, Prince of Peace, and reign!"

Christ Jesus lay in death's strong bands
Martin Luther, 1483-1546. Trans. Richard Massie, 1800-1887
Source: *Enchiridion,* 1524
Luther based his 1524 hymn on the same Latin sequence (Victimae paschali) as the hymn, "Christ is arisen," but after stanza two he created his own masterpiece describing Christ's struggle with death, breaking its power, and bringing us to the festival of gladness at the Easter feast. J.S. Bach's magnificent Cantata 4 on this text highlights the various stanzas with seven different treatments.

Christ the Lord is risen today
Charles Wesley, 1707-1788 and others
Source: *Sacred Poems,* 1739
The standard opening hymn for Easter Sunday is this masterpiece by Charles Wesley. Yet surprisingly his brother John did not include it in his monumental 1780 *Collection of Hymns for the Use of the People Called Methodists.* The florid notes for the Alleluias remind us that sometimes singing moves beyond mere words, adding a larger dimension to our praise.

Christ, whose glory fills the skies
Charles Wesley, 1707-1788
Source: *Hymns and Sacred Poems,* 1740
Wesley's "Morning Hymn" makes no reference to our rest of the night nor the perils of the day ahead, but instead focuses on Christ whose glory fills the skies (Psalm 19:1), who is "the true light" (I John 2:8), the "sun of righteousness" with healing rays (Malachi 3:20), the "dayspring" or dawn chasing the shades of night (Luke 1:78), and the "day star" rising in our hearts (II Peter 1:19). If Christ's presence is with us all of our deepest needs for the day will be met.

Come, Christians, join to sing
Christian Henry Bateman, 1813-1889
Source: *Sacred Melodies for Children,* 1843
The hymn was intended for children, but the second word was changed to "Christians" to make it more universally useful. The very easy tune SPANISH HYMN was arranged by the Philadelphia organist from England who studied with Charles Wesley, Jr. Bateman began as a Moravian minister, then moved to Congregational and finally Anglican parishes.

Come down, O Love Divine
Bianco da Siena, d. 1434

Trans. Richard F. Littledale, 1833-1890
Source: *Laudi Spirituali,* 1851
  This 15th century Italian hymn is an example of pre-Reformation hymns of praise and devotion. Many were written by penitents who, frightened by the devastating wars and plagues of their time, sought atonement for sins by a deeper life of devotion. Vaughan Williams' beautiful hymn tune is perfectly suited to the introspective character of the text.

Come, Holy Ghost, our hearts inspire
Charles Wesley, 1707-1788
Source: *Hymns and Sacred Poems,* 1740
  This is a classic Wesley hymn, to be sung "Before Reading the Scriptures." It is a prayer for illumination of God's Word, which is the source of prophecy, light for our disordered spirits, and love divine. The outline of thought makes it especially suitable for Bible Sunday.

Come, Holy Ghost, our souls inspire
Rhabanus Maurus, c. 776-856. Trans. John Cosin, 1594-1672
Source: Uncertain
  This ninth century hymn has been sung since the 11th century at ordinations, coronations, and confirmation services. The Holy Spirit with creative energy inspires the soul, lightens with celestial fire, imparts the sevenfold gifts (see Revelation 1:4), anoints with unction (oil) to comfort, illuminates our blinded sight, cheers our soiled face, guards us from spiritual foes, and guides our paths. The melody is ancient, having first been associated with an Ambrosian Easter hymn.

Come, labor on
Jane Borthwick, 1813-1897
Source: *Thoughts for Thoughtful Hours,* 1859
  The New Testament passages which liken the winning of souls to the harvesting of grain are the background sources for this hymn. For those who labor faithfully there will be the glad sound at the last, "Well done!" The author, and her younger sister Sarah Findlater, are better known for their 122 translations of German *Hymns from the Land of Luther,* which compare favorably with those of Catherine Winkworth.

Come, let us join our cheerful song
Isaac Watts, 1674-1748
Source: *Hymns and Spiritual Songs,* 1707
  What an exhilarating invitation for the opening of worship — come

and adore the Lamb of God with cheerful song! Watts, called the Father of English Hymnody, captioned the hymn "Christ Jesus, the Lamb of God, Worshipp'd by all the Creation" (Revelation 5:11-13). He is a master at placing joyous, cosmic ideas in simple meters and simple words. Christ is Lord and all creation is called upon to pay Him honor.

Come, my Way, my Truth, my Life
George Herbert, 1593-1632
Source: *The Temple,* 1633
Entitled "The Call," and published posthumously in *The Temple,* this devotional poem for personal use was first included as a hymn in *Songs of Praise,* 1925. The author, a friend of such men as Francis Bacon and King James I, became an Anglican priest, but poor health cut short his career leaving him most famous for his sensitive poetry. The tune, from "Five Mystical Songs," reveals Ralph Vaughan Williams' love for and sensitivity to the author's poetry.

Come, O come, quickening Spirit
Heinrich Held, 1620-1659. Trans. Edward T. Horn, III, b. 1909
Source: *Neuerfundener geistlicher Wasserquelle,* 1658
The author was one of the best of Silesian hymnwriters. To escape Roman Catholic persecutions his family moved to Poland where he learned Polish and studied music. He was successful in poetry, law, government, and hymn writing. His hymn includes elements found in all Pentecost hymns: comfort, light, guidance, deliverance from Satan, and defense.

Come, O thou traveller unknown
Charles Wesley, 1707-1788
Source: *Hymns and Sacred Poems,* 1742
Entitled "Wrestling Jacob," this hymn is an interpretation of Genesis 32:22-30 and Jacob's struggle with the angel to discover the nature of God. Originally in 14 Stanzas, it is an autobiographical description of Wesley's own struggles to find the faith and to learn that God is Love. So great a writer as Isaac Watts said "that single poem, *Wrestling Jacob,* was worth all the verse I myself have written." It should be read thoughtfully and devotionally before it is sung.

Come, risen Lord, and deign to be our guest
George Wallace Briggs, 1875-1959
Source: *Songs of Praise,* 1931
The author, Canon first of Worcester Cathedral and later Leicester Cathedral, entitled this hymn "The Upper Room." It begins with

the Last Supper with Jesus as host, as He is at every communion celebration. Then it moves to the supper at Emmaus (Luke 24:28-35) when Jesus was invited to spend the night with the disciples. At the table Jesus became the host and they the guests!

Come, Thou almighty King
Anon. 18th century
Source: A leaflet published by George Whitefield, n.d.

The hymn has been ascribed to Charles Wesley, but he never wrote anything in this unusual meter, 664. 6664., to which "God save the King" and "My country, 'tis of thee" are sung. It develops a Trinitarian pattern (King – incarnate Word – Holy Comforter) with a closing doxology. The tune was written by the prolific composer, opera conductor, and violinist, Giardini.

Come, thou fount of every blessing
Robert Robinson, 1735-1790
Source: *A Collection of Hymns,* 1759

Born of humble parents, Robinson could not afford schooling for the ministry, so was apprenticed at fourteen to a London barber and hairdresser. After a dissolute youth he was converted by George Whitefield and became a Calvinistic Methodist minister. Like the more famous John Newton's more famous "Amazing grace," his hymn is one of providence and grace. Like Jacob, who raised an Ebenezer (a stone altar which signified that God had brought him thus far), he confesses how great a debtor he is to the grace of God, as are we all.

Come, thou long-expected Jesus
Charles Wesley, 1707-1788
Source: *Hymns for the Nativity of our Lord,* 1744

Although this hymn usually appears in the Advent section, Wesley wrote it for Christmas. Names given for Jesus: strength, consolation, hope, dear desire, and joy. Also note the use of the word "Born" three times to begin lines of poetry in stanza two. The hymn's ultimate emphasis is on the kingship of Jesus, closing with a prayer that Christ will rule in our hearts alone.

Come unto me, ye weary
William C. Dix, 1837-1898
Source: *People's Hymnal,* 1867

All of us at times become weary and discouraged. The comforting invitation of Jesus to "come unto me" and the promise to give us rest, light, and life and never to cast us out was the inspiration for the author's hymn when he was ill and depressed. It is based on Matthew 11:28.

Come, ye faithful, raise the strain
John of Damascus, c. 675-c.749
Trans. John M. Neale, 1818-1866
Source: *Christian Remembrancer,* April 1859

All Greek Easter hymns include references to the Song of Moses (Exodus 15), which is the lesson for the second Sunday after Easter. Deliverance through the Red Sea is related to deliverance by Christ from death. In addition, the hymn uses Spring (the Queen of Seasons) as an allegory of the resurrection. After winter the days grow brighter and warmer, and Christ the Sun of Righteousness returns from the grave to bring us new life and light. For this we give "praise undying."

Come, ye thankful people, come
Henry Alford, 1810-1871
Source: *Psalms and Hymns,* 1844

The title suggests Thanksgiving, but this harvest time is about the final judgment when the good grain will be garnered and the tares thrown into the fire. It is based on Mark 4:26-29 and Matthew 13:36-43. Our prayer is that we will be wholesome and pure grain at the final day of testing.

Comfort, comfort ye my people
Johann Olearius, 1611-1684
Trans. Catherine Winkworth, 1827-1878
Source: *Geistliche Singe-Kunst,* 1671

Based on Isaiah 40:1-5, the text is for Advent but is specially marked for St. John the Baptist's Day, June 24. The author, who was court chaplain at Halle and at one time a member of the philosophy faculty at Wittenberg, included this hymn in his 1671 collection of hymns. The rhythm of the tune suggests a dance for joy at the coming of Christ.

Creater of the stars of night (starry frame; starry height)
Anon. Latin, 9th century. Trans. John Mason Neale, 1818-1866
Source: 9th century ms., Bern

The Latin original, found in a ninth century manuscript in Bern, Switzerland, was appointed to be sung on certain days during Advent. In stanza two there is more than a hint of the hymn "At the name of Jesus." In this hymn the inclusion of a final doxology (a Trinitarian formula of praise) appears for the first time in a Latin hymn.

Creator Spirit, by whose aid
Attr. Rhabanus Maurus, 778-856
Trans. John Dryden, 1631-1700
Source: 11th century ms. earliest written source
  Probably from the ninth century, this famous Pentecost text has been a favorite for translators. Julian in his *Dictionary of Hymnology* listed 35 translations by 1907. One of these was the great English poet, John Dryden, who became Poet Laureate and Historiographer Royal in 1670, but was stripped of these posts when King William (a Protestant) acceded in 1688.

Cross of Jesus, cross of sorrow
William J. Sparrow-Simpson, 1859-1952
Source: *The Crucifixion,* 1887
  The author of the text was responsible for the libretto for John Stainer's "Crucifixion," a Lenten cantata which at one time was immensely popular in England and America. Most of the cantata text is maudlin, but this one hymn has survived, being set either to Stainer's original tune or to the hauntingly beautiful America folk hymn tune, CHARLESTOWN.

Crown Him with many crowns
Matthew Bridges, 1800-1894 and Godfrey Thring, 1823-1903
Source: *Hymns of the Heart,* 1851 and *Hymns and Sacred Lyrics,* 1874
  To illustrate the text, "And on his head were many crowns" (Revelation 19:12), two different authors wrote two different texts, each with six stanzas. Most hymnals make a selection from the twelve stanzas. The tune name DIADEMATA suggests "diadems" or "crowns" and matches the striking first line of poetry with an equally memorable first line of music.

Day is dying in the west
Mary A. Lathbury, 1841-1913
Source: *The Calvary Selection of Spiritual Songs,* 1878
  At Chautauqua in New York at the five o'clock vesper service and again at the evening song service in the amphitheater, this hymn is always sung. The author wrote the hymn in two halves, the first two stanzas in 1877 at the request of the founder of Chautauqua and the last two in 1890. It succeeds in uniting the awesomeness of God's creation with His warm presence at evening. The use of the Sanctus (Holy, holy, holy) for the refrain is most effective textually and vocally.

28

Dear Lord and Father of mankind
John Greenleaf Whittier, 1807-1892
Source: *The Brewing of Soma,* 1872
    Whittier, as a Quaker, never wrote an actual hymn, for he believed in the ideals of simplicity, stillness, and silence. In a poem called *The Brewing of Soma,* after describing the religious frenzy produced by drinking Soma, he prays that God will "forgive our foolish ways." Scriptural allusions are plentiful: disciples rising to follow without a word, Jesus praying in the calm hills, the still small voice of God speaking to Elijah on Mt. Carmel. We can be grateful that a "non-hymn" can be used by singing Christians to provide an insight into spiritual worship.

Dear Master, in whose life I see
John Hunter, 1848-1917
Source: *Monthly Calendar,* Trinity Congregational Church, Glasgow
    If a Scotsman can be thrifty with money, this author is also thrifty with words. In two simple stanzas he forces us to compare ourselves and our shortcomings with the perfection of Christ. We are shamed by the comparison, but pray Christ to guide us until our deeds become closer to our dreams of righteousness.

Dearest Jesus, at your Word
(See: "Blessed Jesus at Thy Word")

Deck thyself, my soul, with gladness
Johann Franck, 1618-1677
Trans. Catherine Winkworth, 1829-1878
Source: *Geistliche Kirchen-Melodien,* 1649
    It is not usual for a burgomaster (mayor) to write hymns, but we are grateful to the famous composer, Johann Crüger, for including this by Mayor Franck in his collection. The hymn celebrates the joy of communion, rather than recalling the passion of Jesus. The famous hymnologist, Julian, says "It is an exhortation to the soul to arise and draw near to partake of the heavenly food and to meditate on the wonders of heavenly love.

Draw nigh (near) and take the body of the Lord
Latin, 7th century. Trans. John M. Neale, 1818-1866
Source: *Antiphonarium Banchoriense,* c. 680-691
    There is a charming Irish legend that this hymn was first sung by angels after St. Patrick and his nephew Sechnall reconciled following an argument. The ancient manuscript (Bangor Antiphonary) was

carried first to Bobbio and then the Ambrosian Library in Milan where it was discovered in the 17th century. The hymn, set in short lines, was commonly sung during the receiving of Communion in Irish churches.

Draw us in the Spirit's tether
Percy Dearmer, 1867-1936
Source: *Songs of Praise,* 1926
This hymn has had a strange career. Dearmer, the English hymnologist and hymnal editor, included it with the initials "B.R." (one of his pseudonyms) as the second part of a hymn by G.H. Bourne, "Lord enthroned in heavenly splendor" in the famous *Songs of Praise.* A popular anthem setting by the late Harold Friedell (1905-1958) was arranged as a hymn by the American Baptist church musician, Jet Turner (1928-1984), for the *Hymnbook for Christian Worship* (1970). The soaring melody is a perfect foil to the romantic and nostalgic text which unites us with the communion of the early disciples.

Earth and all stars
Herbert F. Brokering, b. 1926
Source: *Twelve Folksongs and Spirituals,* 1968
For the 90th anniversary of St. Olaf College in 1964, Brokering, a Lutheran minister and poet, wrote a text which attempts to pick up and praise "many facets of life which merge in the life of the community. So there are references to buildings, nature, learning, family, war, festivity." We can enjoy this contemporary hymn because it brings pictures and visual images to mind as we sing.

Earth has many a noble city
Aurelius Clemens Prudentius, 348-c.413
Trans. Edward Caswall, 1814-1878
Source: *Roman Breviary,* 1632
Imagine singing all 52 stanzas of the original hymn! Pope Pius V in revising the Roman Breviary in 1568 chose four centos, designating them for use in Epiphany. Bethlehem is seen as the noblest of cities because Jesus was born there. The "sacred gifts" of incense, gold and myrrh (this is why some assume "three" kings) point to Christ's divinity, royalty, and mortality.

Eternal Father, strong to save
William Whiting, 1825-1878
Source: *Hymns Ancient and Modern,* 1861
Known as the sailors' hymn, it follows a Trinitarian pattern with

three scriptural bases: Job 38:10, 11 where God prescribes the ocean's boundaries, Matthew 8:23-27 and 14:22-32 Christ stilling the storm and walking on the sea, Genesis 1:2 where the Spirit of God brooded over the face of the deep and created order from chaos. The final stanza is a summary prayer to the Trinity for the safety of sailors — and all of us are sailors on the sea of life.

Eternal God, whose power upholds
Henry Hallam Tweedy, 1868-1953
Source: Hymn Society of America, 1929
This hymn was good enough to be named winner over 1000 other entries in a competition on the theme of missions sponsored by the Hymn Society of America. The powerful use of ''no'' six times in stanza one is followed by stanzas about various attributes of God: love, truth, beauty, righteousness and grace. It is a far cry from the old fashioned mission hymns which saw Americans as Christians and all others as heathen.

Eternal ruler of the ceaseless round
John W. Chadwick, 1849-1904
Source: *A Book of Poems,* 1876
It is difficult in war time to write a hymn which attempts to bridge deep differences. Written for the graduation service at Harvard Divinity School in 1864 at the height of the Civil War, the hymn is a valuable statement for any generation which becomes divided over an important issue. The last stanza, with its ''oneness'' (five times) is the heart of the message, and is well worth some time spent in silent meditation on the theme of peacemaking.

Fairest Lord Jesus
Anon. in a Münster manuscript
Source: *Münster Gesangbuch,* 1677
How often a simple work which no one felt was worth claiming has become an all time favorite. The choir director at St. Thomas' Church in Leipzig (Bach's famous church) discovered the Silesian tune, and Richard Willis (who also wrote the tune for ''It came upon the midnight clear'') introduced it to America. All nature is beautiful, but Jesus is fairest of all.

Faith of our fathers! living still
Frederick W. Faber, 1814-1863
Source: *Jesus and Mary,* 1849
This is a hymn whose focus and meaning is completely different from the intention of the author. Faber sought to convert England

to Catholicism with "Mary's prayers" and "faith of our fathers," but Unitarians altered it for Protestant use, and it is found in practically all American hymnals and sung with enthusiasm as singers vow to be true to the faith till death. God moves in mysterious ways!

Father eternal, ruler of creation
Laurence Housman, 1865-1959
Source: *Songs of Praise,* 1925
We can all find value in many different traditions. Housman's spiritual journey led him through Anglican, Roman Catholic, and Quaker traditions — the last being the root for his pacifist views as stated in this text, written at the close of World War I. The powerful words are a ringing denunciation of the folly of war, with a fervent prayer from the Lord's Prayer ending each stanza.

Father, we praise Thee now the night is over
Attr. to Gregory the Great, 540-604
Trans. Percy Dearmer, 1867-1936
Source: British Museum, 11th century ms.
Written to be sung soon after midnight in monasteries, the text has been altered to make it useful after sunrise — which is a bit more convenient for most of us today. It is in the unusual Sapphic Ode — a combination of three lines of 11 syllables each, followed by a short line of five. Each line begins with the feel of a triplet, and the tune from French sources is most memorable and singable.

Father most holy, merciful, and tender
Latin, 10th century. Trans. Percy Dearmer, 1867-1936
Source: Translation, *English Hymnal,* 1906
Three translations have been made of this sapphic ode text (11.11.11.5.) by A.E. Alston, R.A. Knox, and Percy Dearmer. Two have appeared in Anglican hymnals, and the other in the Catholic *Westminster Hymnal* (1940). The theme is Trinitarian, and phrases of praise and adoration from many sources are borrowed to create a rich tapestry of praise.

Father, we thank Thee, who hast planted
Didache, c. 110. Trans. F. Bland Tucker, 1895-1985
Source: *The Hymnal,* 1940
The *Teaching of the Twelve Apostles* (c. 110) called the *Didache* and discovered in Constantinople, is one of the most important parts of the Communion liturgy. It is a prayer for the whole church, described in the last stanza as grain scattered over the hillsides, but harvested and made into one loaf, bringing to mind the prayer of

Christ to the Father in John 17:21, "That they all may be one." Surely our oneness should be centered in sharing the body and blood of Christ at His table.

Fight the good fight with all thy might
John S. B. Monsell, 1811-1875
Source: *Hymns of Love and Praise,* 1863

Hymn writers often borrow good ideas from others, and it is likely that Monsell got his inspiration from a hymn by James Montgomery called "Valiant for Truth," beginning "Fight the good fight: lay hold upon eternal life." It is thoroughly Biblical: stanza one is based on I Timothy 6:12; stanza two on Hebrews 12:1,2; stanza three on I Peter 5:7; and stanza four on Colossians 3:11. Faith is the hymn's main emphasis, and Christ (name occurs seven times) is the key.

Fling wide the door, unbar the gate
(See: "Lift up your heads, ye mighty gates")

For all the saints, who from their labors rest
William W. How, 1823-1897
Source: *Hymns for a Saint's Day and Other Hymns by a Layman,* 1864

Based on the picture of a "cloud of witnesses" (Hebrews 12:1), the hymn gives thanks for the saints of old, makes a prayer that we may be found faithful, and acknoweldges the unity of the whole Church in heaven and on earth in the mystical body of Christ, a picture of the church in holy warfare, and a vision of the victorious Church. Vaughan Williams' magnificent marching tune makes this a contemporary version of "When the saints go marching in."

For the beauty of the earth
Folliot S. Pierpoint, 1835-1917
Source: *Lyra Eucharistica,* 1864

The original text was intended to show Holy Communion as a joyful, holy feast, and the refrain was "Christ our God, to Thee we raise this our sacrifice of praise." Changing "sacrifice" to "this our hymn" of grateful praise has made it more generally a thanksgiving for creation, for our physical senses, for human love, and for everything good which God gives to us.

For the bread which Thou hast broken
Louis F. Benson, 1855-1930
Source: *Hymns, Original and Translated,* 1925

Dr. Benson was one of America's foremost hymnologists. A Presbyterian minister, he helped edit several hymnals and wrote several books about hymns. The original three stanzas were intended to be sung at the conclusion of the Communion service, but at the suggestion of Henry Sloane Coffin, president of Union Theological Seminary in New York City, a fourth stanza was added relating sacrament to service. The final phrase, taken from the Lord's Prayer, is a most appropriate conclusion to the hymn and the service.

For the fruits of His creation
Fred Pratt Green, b. 1903
Source: *Praise the Lord,* 1972
    This "Harvest Hymn" states several basic themes: thanks for the harvest of nature, a call to share with others and thus do God's will, and thanks for the harvests of the Spirit: goodness, truth and love. The lines beginning "For the wonders that astound us" are a poetical tour de force in terms of ideas and rhymes.

Forgive our sins as we forgive
Rosamund Herklots, b. 1905
Source: Parish Magazine of St. Mary's Church,
    Bromley, Kent, 1966
    There are few hymns which deal with forgiveness. The author has written, "The idea of writing the 'Forgiveness' hymn came to me some years ago when I was digging up docks in a long-neglected garden. Realizing how these deeply-rooted weeds were choking the life out of the flowers in the garden, I came to feel that deeply-rooted resentments in our lives could destroy every Christian virtue and all joy and peace unless, by God's grace, we learned to forgive." This hymn inspires us to be reconciled with each other so that "Our lives will spread your peace."

Forth in Thy name, O Lord, I go
Charles Wesley, 1707-1788
Source: *Hymns and Sacred Poems,* 1749
    Charles wrote hymns for many times and occasion which had never been considered worthy of a hymn, such as "For believers before work." He saw work as a part of Christian service, assigned to us by God. Therefore we should do our work as in God's sight and delight in the opportunity of using the skills given to us. Since every job has its temptations, he wrote another stanza which is almost always omitted: "Preserve me from my calling's snare, And hide my simple heart above, Above the thorns of choking care, The gilded baits of wordly love." Most hymns stick to Sunday — Charles sang about the weekdays as well.

Forty days and forty nights
George Hunt Smyttan, 1822-1870
Source: *Penny Post,* March 1856
The author based his text on Mark 1:12, 13 dealing with Christ's temptation in the wilderness, but seemingly it is concerned chiefly with the physical setting rather than the inner spiritual struggles which are more clearly delineated in the other gospels. It is a useful hymn about the forty days of Lent (Sundays are not counted)!

From all that dwell below the skies
Isaac Watts, 1674-1748, and Anon.
Source: *Psalms of David,* 1719
Based on the two verses that make up the shortest psalm (117), Watts' two stanzas entitled "Praise to God from all Nations" is the first of three versions which he made — in Long Meter, Short Meter, and Common Meter. To the two stanzas John Wesley added two more by an anonymous poet, possibly Robert Spence. Watts' psalm paraphrases set a high standard for later poets.

From heaven above to earth I come
Martin Luther, 1483-1546
Trans. Catherine Winkworth, 1827-1878
Source: *Geistliche Lieder,* 1535
For a family Christmas play Luther wrote a fifteen stanza mini-drama in which his son Hans took the part of the angel in stanzas 1-5, and the family responded with the rest. Luther got his idea from a popular singing game in which a young man would sing a refrain and then give out a riddle to one of the girls in the circle. If she could not solve the riddle she had to give the singer her wreath or garland. The famous tune VOM HIMMEL HOCH was the tune to which this refrain was sung and became the basis for many great organ and choral works.

From Thee all skill and science flow
Charles Kingsley, 1819-1875
Source: *Collected Poems,* 1880
This hymn was either written for the laying of the foundation stone of the workingmen's block of Queen's Hospital in Birmingham, England, or for the opening of the New Wing of the Children's Hospital in the same city — where it was sung by 1000 school children. Whichever is correct, if the first stanza is omitted ("Accept this building") the hymn is more generally sung as a call for us to use skills and science to bring justice to the world.

Gentle Mary laid her child
Joseph Simpson Cook, 1859-1933
Source: *Hymnary of the United Church of Canada,* 1930
This carol was written in 1919 for a competition in Canada, where the author, English born, was a Methodist minister. It retells the Christmas story simply, and has become a favorite because of its marriage to a tune which is usually connected with "Good King Wenceslas," but the melody was written for words about spring.

Gift of Finest Wheat (You satisfy the hungry heart)
Omer Westendorf, b. 1916
Source: *Archdiocese of Philadelphia hymn sheet, 1977*
A Cincinnati Catholic hymnologist-poet joined forces with a Denver composer, Robert E. Kreuz (b. 1922), to write a winning hymn for the Bicentennial Year in 1976. Immediately popular, the hymn has had wide acceptance for Eucharistic celebrations. Although written in changing meters, the natural flow of the melody provides a memorable congregational response, while the choir (or cantor) presents reminders of the many meanings of the celebration of the Lord's Supper. It is designed to be sung during the distribution of the elements.

Give me the wings of faith
Isaac Watts, 1674-1748
Source: *Hymns and Spiritual Songs, 1709*
Watts entitled this hymn "The Examples of Christ and the Saints." After reminding us of the example and testimony of the saints, the author points us to the example of Christ and invites us to follow in his footsteps as we make our way through life to heaven. Watts broke the custom of singing only psalms with his "hymns of human composure" and hymns based on the New Testament.

Give to our God immortal praise
Isaac Watts, 1674-1748
Source: *Psalms of David,* 1719
Based on Psalm 136, with the title "God's wonders of Creation, Providence, Redemption and Salvation," this hymn has been altered to hide the repeating refrain. "Wonders of grace to God belong," which follows the Hebrew pattern of repetition of a line as the basic thrust of the psalm . In the psalm the refrain is "for his steadfast love endures forever."

Give to the winds thy fears
Paul Gerhardt, 1607-1676. Trans. John Wesley, 1703-1791
Source: *Praxis Pietatis Melica,* 1653

Three different authors are involved in this hymn, based on Psalm 37:5 ("Commit thy way unto the Lord; trust also in him; and he shall bring it to pass.") Gerhardt's 12 stanza hymn was based on Martin Luther's translation of the psalm, and John Wesley translated it into English. Would that we could share the kind of faith which Gerhardt had in spite of much suffering and testing. Beneath his portrait in the Lutheran church in Luben, his last pastorate, is the inscription, "A divine sifted in Satan's sieve."

Glories of your name are spoken
(See: Glorious things of Thee are spoken)

Glorious the day when Christ was born
Fred Pratt Green, b. 1903
Source: *Hymns and Songs,* 1967
The author keeps a notebook with full information about every hymn he has written. He acknowledges a debt to Christopher Smart's poem *Song to David* for the appealing start of each stanza, "Glorious the day." The choicest line is "faith achieves what reason planned," teaching us "that the good the world desires can only be achieved through faith—and faith in a religious sense."

Glorious things of Thee are spoken
John Newton, 1725-1807
Source: *Olney Hymns,* 1779
Most classical hymns are Bibically oriented, and this text has references to Isaiah 33:20-21, Psalm 87:3, I Peter 2, Revelation 1, and Exodus 13:22. The author, famous for "Amazing grace," included this in his *Olney Hymns,* written to educate his congregation about the Bible. Like all good hymn writters, Newton knew that hymns are excellent tools for teaching Biblical truth and wisdom, and should be sung with an open and questing mind.

Go, tell it on the mountain
American Folk Hymn
Source: *American Negro Songs and Spirituals,* 1940
It is impossible to pinpoint composers of the melodies of spirituals. Some tunes may have been brought by slaves from Africa, some may have been remolded tunes heard in Baptist and Methodist churches, some may have been imitations of religious songs. Frederick J. Work, probably creator of the words, taught them to the famous Fisk Singers. They are an imperative for us to tell others about Jesus.

Go to dark Gethsemane
James Montgomery, 1771-1854
Source: Cotterill's *Selection,* 1820, and *Christian Psalmist,* 1825
The author actually wrote two different versions of this hymn. Both used vivid language to lead us through the awful events of Christ's suffering — the judgement hall, beatings, climbing Calvary's mountain, the Crucifixion. But then we are called to hasten to the tomb on Easter to meet the risen Christ who overcame all. We too must learn how to pray, to bear the cross, to die to sin, and to rise from death in Christ.

God be with you till we meet again
Jeremiah E. Rankin, 1828-1904
Source: *Gospel Bells,* 1883
What is the origin of the word "Goodbye?" The Congregational pastor from Washington, D.C. originally wrote only the first stanza in 1880 to remind us that it means "God be with you." Later he added 7 more stanzas! A favorite of revivalists, it was carried around the world by the famous team of Dwight L. Moody and Ira D. Sankey.

God hath (has) spoken: by His prophets
George W. Briggs, 1875-1959
Source: *Songs of Faith,* 1945
How does God speak to us? This points to the Bible as the Word of God, spoken through prophets proclaiming an unchanging Word, through Christ — who is the living Word revealing God to us, and through the Spirit — which still speaks every day reminding us that God is the Alpha and Omega, the First and Last. It was one of "Ten New Hymns on the Bible" written for the celebration of the publication of the Revised Standard Version of the Bible in 1952.

God Himself is with us (present)
Gerhard Tersteegen, 1697-1769
Trans. Frederick W. Foster, 1760-1835
Source: *Geistliches Blumen-Gärtlein,* 1729
The author, a mystic who took Christian discipleship seriously, ate only one small meal a day and gave all else to the poor. As a result he suffered poor health and deep depression. He made translations from French mystics and medieval writers, published a hymnal, and gave congregational singing an important place in his ministry. He urged his people "to sing with the spirit of reverence, with sincerity, simplicity and hearty desire" — good advice for us today!

God is love, and where true love (Where charity and love prevail)
Latin Hymn (Carolingian?)
Trans. James Quinn, b. 1919 or Omer Westendorf, b. 1916
Source: *Ancient Anon.*
   Since God is love, we should love one another. The ancient text is most useful for Maundy Thursday, and historically been used in the tradition of washing feet before the celebration of the Last Supper. It is based on I John 4:16.

God is love: let heaven adore Him
Timothy Rees, 1874-1939
Source: *Sermons and Hymns,* 1946
   The author didn't feel his hymn was valuable, but it was found in his papers and sung at his funeral in 1939. The famous *BBC Hymn Book* (can you imagine a CBS, NBC, or ABC hymnal in America?) introduced it, and it has become very popular. The thought outline is clear: God the Creator made everything and loves everyone — there is no one outside the "unfailing grasp." Even when we suffer, God suffers with us. This eternal, unchanging love will hold us to the end, triumphing over sin, death and hell.

God is my strong salvation
James Montgomery, 1771-1854
Source: *Songs of Zion,* 1822
   "The Lord is my light and my salvation; whom then shall I fear?" Psalm 27 is the basis of this hymn by the Moravian minister and newspaper editor who wrote over four hundred hymns. The *Guide to the Pilgrim Hymnal,* 1966, says, "His ear for rhythm was exceedingly accurate and refined. His knowledge of Holy Scripture was most extensive. His religious views were broad and charitable. His devotional spirit was the holiest type." Such a person could hardly fail to be a great hymn writer.

God is working His purpose out
Arthur Campbell Ainger, 1841-1919
Source: Leaflet, 1894. *Foreign Mission Chronicle,* 1900
   This missionary hymn was written in 1894 for the boys of Eton with the refrain, "When the earth shall be filled with the glory of God as the waters cover the sea," based on Isaiah 11:9 and Habakkuk 2:14. There is a stanza often omitted, "What can we do to work God's work." The hymn reminds us that God is the ruler yet and his purposes are being worked out in history day by day.

God moves in a mysterious way
William Cowper, 1731-1800
Source: *Olney Hymns,* 1779

Cowper, befriended by John Newton, went through many periods of doubt and despondency, perhaps made greater by worries over the old fashioned doctrine of predestination. Just as Newton was saved by "grace," Cowper was saved by God's "mercy" as faith and hope were rekindled and he found "Light Shining out of Darkness," as he titled his hymn. God's providence is boundless, but His ways are unfathomable. The text, based on John 13:7, invites us to trust God in all our moments of despair. Routley has called this "undoubtedly one of the great literary classics of hymnody."

God of grace and God of glory
Harry Emerson Fosdick, 1878-1969
Source: *Methodist Hymnal,* 1932

With heavy Rockefeller financial support, Riverside Church in New York was built for Fosdick, one of America's foremost preachers. Non-denominational, the church was opened on October 5, 1930 — a grand occasion which invited self congratulation and more than a little pride. Fosdick faced the time with hopeful enthusiasm but with humility and sometimes fearful apprehension. To mark the occasion he wrote this famous hymn at his summer home in Boothbay Harbor, Maine with its call to face the call of Christ to be disciples, and to pray for wisdom and courage to face the hour, rather than to glory in it.

God of our fathers, whose almighty hand
Daniel C. Roberts, 1841-1907
Source: *The Hymnal,* 1892

Recently America celebrated its 200th birthday. Roberts' hymn was written a century earlier at St. Thomas' Episcopal Church in Brandon, Vermont for the 100th birthday of America. The author served in the Civil War, and spent his years in ministry in small New England parishes. Warren's rousing tune with its trumpet fanfares has helped to make this patriotic text a perennial favorite.

God of our life, through all the circling years
Hugh T. Kerr, 1872-1950
Source: *Hymnal,* 1933 (Presbyterian)

It is all too easy to live only in the present — to forget what we owe the past, and not to put our trust in God for the future. The author, at one time Moderator of the Presbyterian Church, U.S.A. reminds us that our daily pilgrimage is rooted in God who has guided the past, leads us daily, and will give us "our heart's true home when all our years are sped." It is an excellent congregational hymn for use at funerals.

God rest you merry, gentlemen
18th Century English Carol
Source: *Roxburghe Ballads,* c. 1770
   With all traditional carols there is never a known author and never a standard text. The oral tradition hands down the material from singer to singer, and each feels free to take liberties and to make alterations. This is a story carol, and after inviting us to be merry because we have been saved from Satan by Christ's coming, the Christmas story is told. Like many carols, the chorus, or refrain, was for the people to sing after listening to the various stanzas telling the story.

God that madest earth and heaven
Reginald Heber, 1783-1826 and others
Source: *Hymns Written and Adapted to Weekly Services of the Church Year,* 1827
   Sometimes an author's love of a tune triggers words to fit it. This was the case with Heber's love of the Welsh air AR HYD Y NOS. For it he wrote a single stanza as an evening prayer. Three other stanzas have been added by Richard Whateley (Archbishop of Dublin), William Mercer (Anglican vicar) and Frederick Hosmer (American Unitarian), but stanza one is complete in itself.

God the Omnipotent! King, who ordainest
Henry F. Chorley, 1808-1872 and John Ellerton, 1826-1893
Source: Hullah's *Part Music,* 1842 and *Church Hymns,* 1871
   Chorley wrote his text to supply music for the "Russian Hymn," and later Ellerton worte a similar one in imitation, beginning "God the almighty." Both texts pray for the same thing — peace in our time. Editors usually have combined material from both authors. Chorley was a friend of Charles Dickens, and a music critic for the London *Times;* Ellerton was an Anglican priest. Sometimes the press and the church agree to promote the same thing.

God who made the earth and heaven
(See: "God that madest the earth and heaven")

God whose giving knows no ending
Robert L. Edwards, b. 1915
Source: *Ten New Stewardship Hymns,* 1961
   In 1961 the Hymn Society of America was conducting a search

for new hymns on Stewardship. During a summer vacation in the White Mountains of New Hampshire, the author and his family were listening to recordings of hymns and the Welsh tune HYFRYDOL caught his fancy. With this meter in mind he wrote this text which was one of the winning hymns and explains and highlights the meaning of our stewardship of God's resources so graciously given to us.

God, who stretched the spangled heavens
Catherine Arnott Cameron, b. 1927
Source: *Contemporary Worship-I,* 1969

Daughter of the famous New York minister, John Sutherland Bonnell, the author is associate professor of social psychology at the University of La Verne in California. Few hymns speak as eloquently as this about the modern scene. Have we let our inventiveness lead us astray until we are faced with the possibility of self destruction? Has the city become an uncaring place where the lonely drift unnoticed? The hymn ends with a plea to make our work fit into the plans of God. This is one of the finest new hymns of this century.

Good Christian men, rejoice and sing
Cyril A. Alington, 1872-1955
Source: *Songs of Praise,* 1931

The author, former headmaster of Eton and from 1921 chaplain to the king of England, had Vulpius' rousing tune in mind when he wrote this new text for Easter. Few new hymns for that season succeed, but lines such as "the life laid down, the life restored" help to remind us of the eternal freshness of the Easter message.

Good Christian men, rejoice with heart and voice
Latin, 14th Century. Trans. John M. Neale, 1818-1866
Source: *Carols for Christmas,* 1853

When a carol is written in two languages it is called macaronic. The original text was German with snippets of Latin phrases inserted to teach the Christmas story to uneducated people. The music is "foot" music, and obviously was meant to be danced. The church, more accustomed to austere plainsong and motets, decided that the popular music of the day was too good to miss as a teaching tool. As Martin Luther said, "Why should the devil have all the good tunes?"

Great God, we sing that mighty hand
Philip Doddridge, 1702-1751
Source: *Hymns Founded on Various Texts in the Holy Scriptures,* 1755

For a sermon based on Acts 26:22, "Having therefore obtained help of God, I continue unto this day, witnessing both to small and great. . ." for New Year's Day, Doddridge wrote this hymn to be sung following his sermon. The text is filled with many pairs of words and ideas: opening-close, day-night, home-abroad, bounty-counsel, past-future, exalted-depressed, joy-rest. These give a strong sense of the old year passing and the new year beginning.

Great is thy faithfulness
Thomas O. Chisholm, 1866-1960
Source: *Songs of Salvation,* 1923
Many volumes of hymn studies give exotic stories about the origin of gospel songs, but the author wrote in 1955 that there were no special circumstances for his. The Methodist minister gives the "faithfulness of God" as the main theme, and the promise of an unchanging God who assures us of pardon, peace and presence. Its use during the Billy Graham crusades, with its message of great personal comfort have spread its message all over the world.

Guide me, O Thou great Jehovah
William Williams, 1717-1791. Trans. Peter Williams, 1722-1796
Source: *The Hallelujah,* 1745
At the urging of a Welsh evangelist, under whom he was converted, the author began writing hymns as a Welsh Calvinist-Methodist minister. His brother Peter, who was later expelled from the church for heresy, provided the translation. The Exodus and the journey through the wilderness to Canaan is the basis of the hymn with references to "Bread of heaven" (Exodus 16:4-18), "the crystal fountain" (Exodus 17:4-6), "the fiery, cloudy pillar" (Exodus 13:21), "verge of Jordan" (Joshua 3:14-17). The reference to "Death of death and Hell's Destruction" is to Christ (II Timothy 1:10 and Revelation 1:17, 18).

Hail the day that sees Him rise
Charles Wesley, 1707-1788
Source: *Hymns and Sacred Poems,* 1739
This much altered hymn by Charles Wesley is one of the finest for Ascension. It speaks of Christ's work, his triumphal entry into glory, his heavenly reign, and his intercession on our behalf. Although Christ has disappeared from our sight, "Still He calls mankind His own." Christ is still with us!

Hail thee, festival day
Venantius Fortunatus, 535-609. Trans. several, but especially

Percy Dearmer, 1867-1936
Source: *Tempore Florigero,* c. 950
The author was a poet and traveling singer who settled at Poitiers under the influence of Queen Rhadegunda, and was made Bishop of Poitiers in 599. The original had 110 lines of poetry on the Resurrection, and was an Easter poem not designed for singing. It is one of the first to compare the Easter theme to spring and the renewal of nature. During the Middle Ages various sections were used for processionals for festival days, using lines 39 and 40 (Hail thee, festival day) as a refrain.

Hail, Thou once despised Jesus
John Bakewell, 1721-1819 and Martin Madan, 1726-1790
Source: *A Collection of Hymns Addressed to the HOLY, HOLY, HOLY Triune God,* 1757
The author, who lived to be 98 (our longest lived hymn writer), was an English Methodist minister in whose home Thomas Olivers wrote "The God of Abraham praise." To the original two stanzas, others were added by Madan, who became chaplain to the Lock Hospital (an institution for the "restoration of unhappy females.") It can best be described as rhymed theology, and is intended for Ascensiontide.

Hail to the Lord's anointed
James Montgomery, 1771-1854
Source: *Evangelical Magazine,* 1822
Like Watts' "Jesus shall reign," this hymn is a free paraphrase of Psalm 72, but it keeps closer to the biblical text. It was introduced to the South Seas by a Moravian missionary, after having first been sung at Christmas, 1821, at a Moravian settlement in England. The righteous reign of the Lord offers aid to the poor and oppressed, and brings peace and prosperity to the nation. It ends with a vision of a universal and eternal reign — "His name shall stand forever." That name is "Love" — a theme which he probably borrowed from the Wesleys, whom he admired.

Hark! a thrilling voice is sounding
Latin, 5th century (?). Trans. Edward Caswall, 1814-1878
Source: Recast in *Roman Breviary,* 1632
The text, dubiously ascribed to Ambrose, is based on Romans 13:11 and Luke 21:25, and is one of the standard hymns for Advent. The word "thrilling" originally was "awful," then changed to "herald." Caswall's translations are considered to be second only to those of John Mason Neale. After his wife's death he devoted himself to cler-

ical duties, service to the poor and sick, and to writing devotional materials and translating Latin hymns.

Hark, the glad sound, the Savior comes
Philip Doddridge, 1702-1751
Source: *Hymns Founded on Various Texts in the Holy Scriptures,* 1755

For the theme "Christ's message" based on Luke 4:18-19 ("The Spirit of the Lord is upon me, because he hath anointed me to preach the gospel to the poor. . .") the author wrote a seven stanza hymn, which is always shortened in modern hymnals. The author, one of 20 children, was an Independent (Congregational) minister. He also founded an academy where he taught Hebrew, Greek, philosophy, logic, algebra, trigonometry, and theology. From over work he died of tuberculosis.

Hark! the herald angels sing
Charles Wesley, 1707-1788
Source: *Hymns and Sacred Poems,* 1739

The original first line was "Hark, how all the welkin rings, Glory to the King of kings." Since "welkin" (all the heavens) was obscure, the line was changed by the famous preacher George Whitefield. This is the most theological of our Christmas hymns, and owes much of its popularity to the tune of Mendelssohn , taken from his cantata for male voices and brass choir celebrating the invention of printing by Gutenberg. He wrote, "I am sure that piece will be liked very much by the singers and the hearers, but it will *never* do to sacred words." How wrong he was! The tune that Wesley had in mind was EASTER HYMN, to which we sing "Jesus Christ is risen today."

Have faith in God, my heart
Bryn Austin Rees, 1911-1983
Source: *Congregational Praise,* 1951

The text was submitted unsolicited to the editorial committee of *Congregational Praise.* It is profoundly simple, weaving a call to have faith in heart, mind and soul. The last stanza ties it all together neatly by repeating these three words. A Congregational minister, Rees has held pastorates in Hertfordshire, Suffolk, and London.

Have thine own way, Lord
Adelaide Addison Pollard, 1862-1934
Source: *Northfield Hymnal,* 1907

The author was born in Bloomfield, Iowa, studied in Boston, taught in a girls' school in Chicago, and taught eight years at the Missionary Training School in Nyack-on-the-Hudson, New York. The hymn was written in 1902 following a Prayer Meeting and when she had been suffering "great distress of soul." Along with an evangelist named Sandford she had attempted unsuccessfully to finance a missionary trip to Africa. The text is a classic statement of acquiescence to the will of God.

He leadeth me: Oh, blessed thought!
Joseph Henry Gilmore, 1834-1918
Source: *Watchman and Reflector,* 1864
Wives are often looking out for their husbands without the men's knowledge! The author wrote this text for a lecture on Psalm 23 for a midweek prayer service at First Baptist Church in Philadelphia, and Mrs. Gilmore sent it to a Boston paper where it was first published without the author's knowledge. It was the composer, William Bradbury, who added the refrain, making this a most popular hymn with its comforting message of God's hand leading us in every circumstance. "He leadeth me" is drawn from Psalm 23.

He who would valiant be
John Bunyan, 1628-1688. Alt. by Percy Dearmer, 1867-1936
Source: *Pilgrim's Progress, Pt. II,* 1684
John Bunyan in his famous opus, written largely in prison, after a conversation between Great-Heart and Valiant-for-Truth, sums up what is required of a pilgrim. Originally it began "Who would true Valour see, Let him come hither." Dearmer, the famous English hymnal editor, thought that Bunyan would never have permitted the original form (with its reference to hobgoblins and foul fiends) as a hymn; therefore he revised it, and American hymnals have opted for the revision while the British sing the original.

Herald, sound the note of judgment
Moir A. J. Waters, 1906-1980
Source: *Hymn Book (Canadian),* 1971
The distinguished Canadian author was born in India, studied and was ordained in Canada, served churches in Scotland and Canada before returning as a missionary to India. He was a popular radio pulpiteer in British Columbia. The hymn was written for the dedication of a new window at Robinson Memorial Church in London, Ontario, with the subject of Jesus' baptism. The text reflects John the Baptist as the herald trumpet prophesying Christ as foretold in Isaiah 40:3 ("A voice cries: In the wilderness prepare the way of the Lord.")

Here, O my Lord, I see Thee face to face
Horatius Bonar, 1808-1899
Source: *Hymns of Faith and Hope,* 1857
Among the some 100 poems which Bonar wrote, this hymn written for a communion service at the request of his elder brother is
the only one in regular usage in America. Bonar presents the sacrament as a place where we meet our living Lord. By faith we see him
"face to face," "touch and handle things unseen," "feed upon the
bread of God," and "drink the royal wine of heaven." All this makes
the sacrament a very personal encounter with Christ.

Holy God, we praise Thy name
Ignaz Franz, 1719-1790
Source: *Katholische Gesangbuch,* 1774
The early church "Te Deum Laudamus" is one of the great hymns
of praise, creed, and supplication. Written in 1774, Franz's hymn
is a German paraphrase of the "Te Deum." Written for a Catholic
hymnal, it is equally loved and sung by Protestants to the German
melody GROSSER GOTT, which is also the basis for the shorter
tune sung to "Sun of my soul." The hymn was played as President
Kennedy's casket was carried out of St. Matthew's Cathedral in
Washington, D.C.

Holy, holy, holy! Lord God almighty
Reginald Heber, 1783-1826
Source: *Selection of Psalms and hymns for the Parish Church,*
    Banbury, 1827
In spite of a very limited rhyme scheme (the "ee" vowel), irregular accent, and uneven numbers of syllables in the various lines, this
hymn based on John's vision of God enthroned in heavenly glory
as found in Revelation 4 is a very popular hymn. The use of the angels'
song (Holy, holy, holy) is pure adoration of God in his "wholly-
otherness." Although filled with apocalyptic language, the hymn
combines a sense of mystery with God's mercy, power, love and
purity.

Holy Spirit, Truth divine
Samuel Longfellow, 1819-1892
Source: *Hymns of the Spirit,* 1864
Two Samuels (Longfellow and Johnson) edited *Hymns of the Spirit,*
1864, for Unitarians. The hymn was headed "Prayer for Inspira-
tion," and is a prayer for truth to dawn, love to glow, power to fill
and nerve, and right to reign — instead of the usual address to the
Holy Spirit as a part of the Trinity.

Hope of the world, Thou Christ of great compassion
Georgia Harkness, 1891-1965
Source: *Eleven New Ecumenical Hymns,* 1954
"Hope of the World" indicates how Christ manifests himself to the world by God's authority. The text, by noted theologian Georgia Harkness, was the winning hymn in the 1953 Hymn Society of America search for new texts on the theme "Jesus Christ, Hope of the World." This was the theme of the 1954 World Council of Churches Assembly in Evanston, Illinois. Since that time it has appeared in every major hymnal. There is hope for the world!

Hosanna, loud hosanna
Jeannette Threlfall, 1821-1880
Source: *Sunshine and Shadow,* 1873
The author, daughter of a Blackburn, England wine merchant, was lamed and disfigured early in life by an accident, and in another was lamed for life. With much time on her hands, she turned to writing hymns which she sent anonymously to various periodicals. This hymn, based on Mark 11:1-10 for Palm Sunday is widely used in church schools.

How brightly shines the morning star
(O Morning Star, how fair and bright)
Philipp Nicolai, 1556-1608
Trans. Catherine Winkworth, 1827-1878
Source: *Frewden Spiegel,* 1599
Called the "Queen of the Chorales" (the King is "Wake, awake, for night is flying"), the words and melody were written by the pastor in Westphalia under the title "A Spiritual bridal song of the believing soul, concerning her Heavenly Bridegroom, founded on the 45th Psalm of the Prophet David." Although the meter is exotic, there is much repetition of melodic material which makes the tune easy to learn and remember. It is a popular hymn for Lutheran weddings.

How firm a foundation
"K" in John Rippon *A Selection of Hymns,* 1787
Since Richard Keen was the precentor (song leader) in Dr. Rippon's church in London, it is reasonable to assume that he was the author. There are many Scriptural references: Isaiah 43:1-5, 12; II Timothy 2:19, and Hebrews 13:5. It is basically about the promises of God, and hymnals use quotation marks for all of the stanzas in which various promises are quoted. The last line, "I'll never, no never, no, never forsake!" is a triumphant conclusion.

How gentle God's commands

Philip Doddridge, 1702-1751
Source: *Hymns Founded on Various Texts in the Holy Scriptures*, 1755
    The author, a friend and great admirer of Isaac Watts, served for 22 years as minister of the Nonconformist chapel at Castle Hill,Northampton. To educate his poor parishioners he founded an academy, producing many who became Congregational ministers. His 400 hymns were all published after his death. They were lined out from a single copy by the precentor and repeated by the congregation. This hymn was sung following his sermon based on I Peter 5:7 ("Cast all your care on him; for he carest for you."").

How Great Thou Art (O Lord, my God! When I in awesome wonder)

Carl Boberg, 1859-1940. Trans. Stuart K. Hine, 1899-
Source: *Mönsteras Tidningen*, 1886
    It would take the FBI to trace the history of this popular hymn. Written in Sweden as a poem, it came to be sung to a popular Swedish melody, moved next to Germany but translated there by an Estonian, then to Russia where it was published in 1927. Stuart Hine, who settled in the Western Ukraine, brought out an English translation which contains little of the nine stanza original, but his setting has become an all time favorite due to its use in the Billy Graham crusades.

How sweet the name of Jesus sounds

John Newton, 1725-1807
Source: *Olney Hymns*, 1779
    Newton titled this hymn "The Name of Jesus," and based it on Song of Solomon 1:3. Stanzas one and two list seven things which Jesus' name does. Stanza three gives ten names for Jesus. Charles Wesley also wrote a great hymn on the name of Jesus ("Thou hidden source of calm repose"). You may find it interesting to compare the two different approaches to the name of Jesus (which means "He will save his people.")

I bind unto myself today

Attr. St. Patrick, c. 372-466. Trans. Cecil F. Alexander, 1823-1895
Source: 11th century manuscripts
    This famous text has been attributed to St. Patrick as sung to the tune "Breastplate," an ancient Irish tune. The fanciful legend tells of Druid worship, lighting a Paschal fire on the Hill of Slane to con-

found the Druid king Loegaire, Patrick and his followers being transformed into deer and escaping. The preface to the hymn in the 11th century manuscript says, "It is a lorica of faith for the protection of body and soul against demons and men and vices: when any person shall recite it daily with pious meditation on God, demons shall not dare to face him, it shall be a protection to him against all poison and envy, and it shall be a guard to him against sudden death, it shall be a lorica for his soul after decease." All very magical!

I come with joy to meet my Lord
Brian Wren, b. 1936
Source: July 1968 service at Hockley, England

It is rare that a new hymn becomes immediately popular, but Wren's simple words suggesting important theological themes is an example. Written to sum up a series of sermons on the meaning of communion, it begins with the personal "I" but ends with the corporate "Together met, together bound, *we'll* go our different ways." As we share the Lord's table we are bound in fellowship, but then must go out into the world to "live and speak his praise."

I heard the voice of Jesus say
Horatius Bonar, 1808-1889
Source: *Hymns, Original and Selected,* 1846

Titled "The Voice from Galilee," the hymn centers on three of the sayings of Jesus found in John 1:16, Matthew 11:28, and John 4:14, John 8:12. The first half of each stanza gives Jesus' invitation, and the second half gives the response of the author — and our response as well.

I know not how that Bethlehem's Babe
Harry Webb Farrington, 1879-1931
Source: *Rough and Brown,* 1921

A prize was offered in 1910 at Harvard University for a Christmas hymn, and Farrington, a first year graduate student, was the winner. We may not understand all of the theological jargon or the mysteries of "Incarnation," "Atonement," and "Salvation," but we do know what Christ means to us personally; and that is the most important thing about our faith. We may not comprehend the one, but we have experienced the other.

I know that my Redeemer lives
Samuel Medley, 1738-1799
Source: *Psalms and Hymns, Extracted from Different Authors,*
  1775

There are four different hymns that begin with this first line, but the most famous is by a former British sailor, converted by reading a sermon by Isaac Watts and then serving as a Baptist minister. Thirteen times he repeats the phrase, "He lives!", making a great crescendo of the passage from Job 19:25, "I know that my Redeemer lives" — the heart of the Easter message.

I love Thy kingdom, Lord
Timothy Dwight, 1752-1817
Source: *The Psalms of David,* 1801
Based on verses five and six of Psalm 137, this is perhaps the oldest hymn written by an American which has remained in continuous use, the only one of 33 by the grandson of Jonathan Edwards and president of Yale University to survive. It was included in his revision of Isaac Watts' *Psalms of David,* needed to remove British references unacceptable in the newly formed United States of America. It expresses a love for the church which congregations feel and wish to express.

I love to tell the story
Katherine Hankey, 1834-1911
Source: *Joyful Songs,* 1869
Many people sing this hymn vigorously but do little to go out and "tell the story" beyond the church walls. Kate Hankey startled England by the unheard-of thing by starting a Bible class for working girls in London. She also served as a nurse in South Africa, and turned over all proceeds from her writings to Christian missions. She lived what she wrote!

I need Thee every hour
Annie S. Hawks, 1835-1918
Source: *Royal Diadem,* 1872
The hymn was written for a Convention of National Baptist Sunday School Association in Cincinnati in 1871. Based on John 15:5 ("I am the vine, you are the branches. . . .") it reminds us that we cannot go it alone — that we are dependent on Christ every moment of our life, whether in temptation, joy or pain.

I sing a song of the saints of God
Lesbia Scott, 1898-1986
Source: *Everyday Hymns for Children,* 1929
Are there any saints living today? The author's three children often asked such questions, and this hymn was written for All Saints' Day (Nov. 1), to suggest that there are plenty of saints alive today in all

sorts of jobs — and that anyone can be a saint if we really work at it. The tune GRAND ISLE has just the light-hearted, joyful feeling to fit the disarmingly simple and picturesque text. To really enjoy it, become as a child!

I sing th' almighty power of God
Isaac Watts, 1674-1748
Source: *Divine Songs Attempted in Easy Language, for the Use of Children,* 1715
It is rare that a profound theologian and hymn writer can write well for children, but at least in this one hymn Watts succeeded. His collection was the first hymnal written exclusively for children. The words are filled with vivid pictures of the handiworks of God, and remind us that God is everywhere in our midst. (It is alright for adults to sing this, too!)

I sought the Lord, and afterward I knew
Anonymous
Source: *Holy Songs, Carols and Sacred Ballads,* 1889
"He first loved us." This simple, yet profound, thought is the basis for the hymn. God loved us long before we knew it. We seek God, but already God is holding out a hand waiting for us to take hold of it and be rescued from the seas of life. Because of the unusual meter, it may be that this is more useful as a poem than as a hymn, but it can be a powerful guided meditation.

I to the hills will lift mine eyes
Psalm 121
Source: The *Scottish Psalter,* 1650
It seems that Presbyterians have always been the strong supporters of psalm singing. John Calvin's *Genevan Psalter,* Sternhold and Hopkins *Old Version,* Tate and Brady's *New Version,* collections by Rous, Barton, Boyd (even King James I of England) — all were distilled into the famous *Scottish Psalter* of 1650. From this book the versions of Psalm 23 and 121 have survived — classics which rank with the King James Version of the Bible, and *The Book of Common Prayer.*

If thou but suffer God to guide thee
George Neumark, 1621-1681. Trans. Catherine Winkworth, 1827-1878
Source: *Fortgepflanzter musikalisch-poetischer Lustwald,* 1657
Based on Psalm 55:22 ("Cast thy burden on the Lord, and he shall sustain thee,") this hymn reminds us that God will care for and

preserve his own in his own time. It does not promise that evil will never befall us, but it does promise to provide us with the strength to carry us through the evil days. Trust and faith in such times are difficult, but God will not forsake us in our time of need.

If you but trust in God to guide you.
(See: "If thou but suffer God to guide thee")

I'll praise my Maker while I've breath
Isaac Watts, 1674-1748. Altered by John Wesley, 1703-1791
Source: *Psalms of David, Imitated in the Language of the New Testament,* 1719
Watts wrote two versions of Psalm 146 with much the same words but in two different meters. Wesley chose the second and made a few alterations and omissions of stanzas. It was one of his favorites and he sang it, instead of any hymn by his brother Charles, as he lay dying. Although it begins with God of creation, it ends with concern for the blind, the troubled, strangers, widows, fatherless children and prisoners. God whose concern reaches to everyone is worthy of praise, in this life and the life to come.

Immortal, invisible, God only wise
Walter Chalmers Smith, 1824-1908
Source: *Hymns of Christ and the Christian Life,* 1867
"Now unto the King eternal, immortal, invisible, the only wise God, be honor and glory forever and ever" (I Timothy 1:17) is the basis for this hymn of pure praise. The rollicking anapestic rhythm of the Welsh melody rushes the singer along to the climactic poetic thought of God being invisible only because He is hidden by the splendor of light.

Immortal love, forever full
John Greenleaf Whittier, 1807-1892
Source: *Tent on the Beach and Other Poems,* 1867
Sometimes the "untraditional" Christian poet expresses our human needs better than the "professional" religionist. The Quaker poet's hymn was taken from a 38 stanza poem called "Our Master," and reminds us that Christ is always near us: in the press of the crowd, by beds of pain, and at our death. Such a love flows freely to each one of us as a never ebbing sea.

In Adam we have all been one
Martin H. Franzmann, 1907-1976
Source: *A New Song,* 1963

Franzmann, author of many theological and devotional books, and Missouri Synod Lutheran representative to the Lutheran World Federation in 1962, has written a powerful exposition of our sinful following the example of Adam. Yet the new Adam, Christ, has loved us and saved us if we turn to Him. The hymn ends with a prayer for the Holy Spirit to set us free from sinning.

In Christ there is no east or west
John Oxenham, 1852-1941 (pen name for William Arthur
   Dunkerley)
Source: *Bees in Amber,* 1913
   The text was written for a pageant presented by the London Missionary Society and is an example of a prophetic hymn — one that states the ideal to be achieved rather than the present situation. Unity and mission are combined, for the mark of a disciple is love for every person and the willingness to serve all humankind.

In heavenly love abiding
Anna L. Waring, 1823-1910
Source: *Hymns and Meditations by A. L. W.* 1850
   This is a gentle setting of Psalm 23:4 ("I will fear no evil, for Thou are with me"), entitled "Safety in God." There is a serene confidence in God's unchanging love, constant presence, and watchful care — the very things which make the 23rd Psalm the number one favorite. In the last line the word "treasure" refers to our heart, suggesting that God wants our supreme love.

In memory of the Savior's love
Thomas Cotterill, 1779-1823. St. 2 Anon.
Source: *A Selection of Psalms and Hymns for Public and Private Use,* 1805
   The title, "For the Sacrament," suggests the theme of the hymn, which originally began "Bless'd with the presence of their God." Everyone is welcome at the Lord's table where we become one in fellowship, faith, and hope with one Lord and one God. It is by faith that we celebrate now and look forward to the celebration at the feast in heaven. The author published a hymnal in 1810 which resulted in a lawsuit trying to declare the use of hymns in church to be illegal — a lawsuit which mercifully failed and opened the way for a wide range of hymns to be sung in church.

In the bleak midwinter
Christina G. Rossetti, 1830-1894
Source: *Scribner's Monthly,* January 1872

Like many Christmas songs written in the Victorian era, this hymn assumes English surroundings and weather. While it is possible there may have been snows in Bethlehem, the secret of the hymn lies elsewhere in the sensitive and imaginative expression of the Incarnation. Set to a musical gem by the famous composer, Gustav Holst, in the 1906 *English Hymnal*, it is a perennial favorite at Christmas.

In the cross of Christ I glory
John Bowring, 1792-1872
Source: John Bowring, 1825
   The theme was suggested by Galatians 6:14 ("But God forbid that I should glory, save in the cross of our Lord Jesus Christ.") The author, a Unitarian, claimed to know 200 languages and to speak 100. At one time he was Governor of Hong Kong. History is littered with civilizations and empires which have risen and fallen, but the cross has outlived them all. The cross also has deep meaning for us personally, giving us peace and joy in times of crises and disappointments.

In the hour of trial
James Montgomery, 1771-1854. Alt. Frances A. Hutton, 1811-1877
Source: *Original Hymns for Public, Private, and Social Devotion,* 1853
   In Luke 22:32, Jesus told Peter that he had prayed for him, that his faith not fail. We all know that his faith did fail and that he betrayed Jesus, but we also know that Peter became one of the founders of the church. So Montgomery gives us a prayer to sing to Jesus, asking that we not fail in our times of trial and temptation; and finally asking that Jesus will be our advocate in that final day of judgment.

Infant holy, infant lowly
Polish Carol. Paraphrased E. M. C. Reed, 1885-1933
Source: *Music and Youth,* 1924
   Many Christmas carols are based on dance rhythms, and this is in the form of a Polish mazurka with its strong downbeat, made famous by Chopin. The many short lines of four syllables with constant rhyming add to the charm of the Christmas story told in simple folk style set to a tune with irresistable melodic sequences.

It came upon the midnight clear
Edmund Hamilton Sears, 1810-1876
Source: *Christian Register,* 1849
   The Unitarian minister who wrote this hymn was deeply involved

in the "'social gospel,'" and his hymn is the first to include the social dimensions of what it means to work for "peace on earth and good will towards men.'' Based on Luke 2:13-14, it is a call for us to respond to the song of the angels and to send back to heaven the message that we will make peace on earth. Unfortunately, after 2000 years we still cannot report much progress.

It happened on that fateful night
Isaac Watts, 1674-1748
Source: *Hymns and Spiritual Songs,* 1709
The first line originally was " 'Twas on that dark and doleful night.'' Whether we sing "fateful" or "doleful,'' the night of Christ's betrayal and arrest is one of the dark moments of history. Yet the focus of this hymn is on the Supper with the disciples which preceded the event and foreshadowed the sacrifice Christ was to make. Each time we celebrate this feast we show forth Christ's death and resurrection and look forward to the final feast of gladness with Christ in heaven.

Jerusalem, my happy home
Anonymous
Source: F. B. P. based on *Liber Meditationum,* 1553
Several different sources have been found for this text, but it would seem that it may be by Francis Baker (Roman Catholic Priest) who based it on a meditation by Augustine on the hoped for peace of Jerusalem, the holy city of heaven where all will be peace and joy. Like many "old fashioned'' texts, it owes its present popularity to the delightful early American folk tune, LAND OF REST.

Jerusalem the golden
Bernard of Cluny, 12th Century.
Trans. John Mason Neale, 1818-1866
Source: *De Contemptu Mundi,* 12th century
Imagine writing a poem of 2,966 lines in dactylic hexameters (six groups of triplets) with inner rhyme, to describe the evils and vices (including those of the church) of the times. Bernard remarked, "Unless the Spirit of wisdom and understanding had flowed in upon me, I could not have put together so long a work in so difficult a meter.'' Neale's translation of a very small portion of the long poem directs our thoughts toward heaven and encourages us to keep striving to reach that marvelous country.

Jesus calls us: O'er the tumult
Cecil Frances Alexander, 1818-1895

Source: *Hymns for Public Worship,* 1852
"A namby-pamby, childish style is most unpleasing to children.
It is surprising how soon they can understand and follow a high order
of poetry." Thus wrote Cecil Frances Alexander, author of the hymn
"Jesus calls us." She was a 19th century educator in her native Ireland
and wrote many hymns for children to illuminate and expand the
Catechism — on Baptism, the Creed, the Commandments, Prayer
and the Lord's Supper. This hymn is for St. Andrew's day.

Jesus Christ is risen today
Latin, 14th Century
Source: *Lyra Davidica,* 1708
    A five stanza Easter carol which first appeared in German and
Bohemian manuscripts of the 14th century was translated in *Lyra
Davidica,* but in John Arnold's 1749 *The Complete Psalmodist* only
the first stanza was retained and others substituted for the original.
In the same meter as Wesley's "Christ the Lord is risen today,"
it is made up of a series of short one-liners which are easy to remem-
ber, and with added Alleluias it is a favorite Easter hymn.

Jesus lives! The vict'ry's won!
Christian Fürchtegott Gellert, 1715-1769
Trans. Frances E. Cox, 1812-1897
Source: *Geistlichen Oden und Lieder,* 1757
    Because preaching from a manuscript was forbidden and Gellert
didn't trust his memory, he became a popular teacher of young
students, noted for his spirited and humorous fables. His hymn is
about the confidence which we all can have because "Jesus lives!,"
and shows his skills in theology, philosophy, poetry and rhetoric.

Jesus, lover of my soul
Charles Wesley, 1707-1788
Source: *Hymns and Sacred Poems,* 1740
    John Wesley omitted this hymn from his famous 1780 collection
because he felt "lover of my soul" was too intimate, proving that
not every hymn will be equally liked by everyone. If we know that
Charles used the heading "In Temptation" we can begin to understand the depth of intensity of the text. If we turn to Jesus for strength
when we are tempted to sin, he will help us to overcome. We are
reminded of the phrase, "Lead us not into temptation, but deliver
us from evil" from the Lord's Prayer.

Jesus, priceless treasure
Johann Franck, 1618-1677

Trans. Catherine Winkworth, 1827-1878
Source: *Praxis Pietatis Melica,* 1653
   A love song by H. Alberti, "Flora meine Freude, meiner Seele
Weide," was the inspiration for this song of love to Jesus. Because
Jesus is our treasure, our pleasure, our friend, we will not be sad
and will find peace in the storms of life. The author wrote 100 pietistic
hymns, although he was primarily a lawyer and government official.

Jesus, refuge of the weary
Girolamo Savonarola, 1472-1498
Trans. Jane F. Wilde, 1826-1986
Source: *Laudi Spirituali,* 1563
   The author intended a medical profession, but the cultural upheaval
of the Italian Renaissance turned him to monastic life where he spent
his energies fighting the intrusion of pagan philosophies from Plato,
Seneca and Ovid into the Christian church. His *Laudi Spirituali* were
written to combat and replace objectionable secular songs in church
use at the time. He condemned the immorality and worldliness of
Pope Alexander VI, and his powerful influence over the populace
of Florence incurred the wrath of both the Pope and the city officials.
He was condemned a heretic, hanged, and his body burned May 23,
1498.

Jesus, Savior, pilot me
Edward Hopper, 1816-1888
Source: *Sailor's Magazine,* 1871
   The author was Presbyterian pastor of the Church of the Sea and
Land in New York City, where many in his congregation were sailors.
Using pictures of life on the sea, he includes the story of Jesus com-
manding the waves "to be still." The last stanza uses the picture
of death as landing on the other shore after crossing the treacherous
waters of this life.

Jesus shall reign where'er the sun
Isaac Watts, 1674-1748
Source: *Psalms of David, Imitated in the Language of the New
   Testament,* 1719
   This is a paraphrase of the second part of Psalm 72, entitled
"Christ's Kingdom among the Gentiles." A missionary hymn, it was
written fifty years before the birth of the modern missionary move-
ment. Here is an example of Christianizing the psalms, for there was
no doubt in Watts' mind that the "King" of the psalm was Christ,
whose kingdom would stretch around the world.

Jesus, still lead on
Nikolaus Ludwig von Zinzendorf, 1700-1760
Trans. Jane L. Borthwick, 1813-1897
Source: *Sammlung, 1725 Geistlicher und lieblicher Lieder*

It was Zinzendorf who gave shelter to the Moravians (Hussites) fleeing persecution, and who helped to establish the famous colonies in Bethlehem, PA and Salem, NC. John Wesley was attracted to his hymns and made a translation, "O Thou, to whose all-searching sight" known by Methodists. Jane Borthwick's version emphasizes the same theme of trust and faith in following Jesus on our way to heaven — our Fatherland.

Jesus, the very thought of Thee
Attr. to Bernard of Clairvaux, 1091-1153.
Trans. Edward Caswall, 1814-1878
Source: Latin manuscript, 13th Century

From 43 stanzas, two Communion hymns have been extracted — this and "Jesus thou joy of loving hearts." It was customary to write long meditations for use during the Sacrament or for seasons of penitence. The words are passionately addressed to Jesus, reflecting an intensity of devotion which is all too rare today.

Jesus, Thou joy of loving hearts
Attr. to Bernard of Clairvaux, 1091-1153
Trans. Ray Palmer, 1808-1887
Source: *The Sabbath Hymn Book,* 1858

Palmer, one of America's earliest and finest hymn writers, chose stanzas from the 42 by Bernard for a devotional hymn which is not specifically for communion except for one stanza ("We taste Thee, O Thou living bread"). Christ is the focal point as the fountain of life and the light of the world.

Jesus, Thy boundless love to me
Paul Gerhardt, 1607-1676. Trans. John Wesley, 1703-1791
Source: *Praxis Pietatis Melica,* 1653

This hymn by the second greatest German Lutheran hymn writer after Martin Luther, found in the Moravian *Herrnhut Gesangbuch* (1735), translated in Georgia by the English founder of Methodism, John Wesley, was entitled "Living by Christ." It represents the yearning of all Christians to place Christ at the center of our lives.

Joy to the world, the Lord is come
Isaac Watts, 1674-1748
Source: *The Psalms of David, Imitated in the Language of the*

New Testament, 1719

Entitled "The Messiah's Coming and Kingdom" and based on the second half of Psalm 98, the hymn is representative of Watts' ability to Christianize the psalms. While it is usually sung at Christmas, the text is actually appropriate to the entire year whenever the theme of the "Kingdom" is observed. The early American church musician, Lowell Mason, arranged a melody from George F. Handel (possibly from "The Messiah") which expressed the joy of the text.

Joyful, joyful we adore Thee
Henry Van Dyke, 1852-1933
Source: *Poems,* 1911

Since the last movement of Beethoven's Ninth Symphony (The Choral) used Schiller's secular text, "Ode to Joy," the author (while visiting Williams College and admiring the Berkshire mountains) composed sacred words with the admonition, "It must be sung to the music of Beethoven's 'Hymn to Joy'." The result is one of the most popular of American hymns.

Judge eternal, throned in splendor
Henry S. Holland, 1847-1918
Source: *Commonwealth,* 1902

This was the author's only hymn, but what a magnificent statement of social concern for the nation! Written at a time of national unrest in England, it is still appropriate today in its call for God to purge the nation of "bitter things" and to cleanse "through the glory of the Lord."

Just as I am, without one plea
Charlotte Elliott, 1789-1871
Source: *Hours of Sorrow, Cheered and Comforted,* 1836

The author became a semi-invalid at 32 and felt her life was useless. A visiting Swiss evangelist, Dr. Cesar Malan, asked her if she were a Christian — a question which she (as daughter of a clergyman) resented and told him so. Later she apologized and said she did not know how to come to Christ. "Come to him just as you are," was the answer. Twelve years later she wrote this highly personal witness to salvation.

Lamp of our feet, whereby we trace
Bernard Barton, 1784-1849
Source: *The Reliquary,* 1849

From the longest Psalm (119) the author chose verse 105, "Thy word is a lamp unto my feet, and a light unto my path," as the basis for the hymn. However, he enlarged it to include other figures of speech: lamp, path, stream, brook, bread, manna, guide, Word, and will — with a final prayer that we learn with simple, child-like hearts.

Lead, kindly light, amid the encircling gloom
John Henry Newman, 1801-1890
Source: *British Magazine,* 1834
   Newman grappled for many years with deep religious questions, which eventually led him from the Anglican Church to the Church of Rome. His hymn was written on a becalmed ship in the Mediterranean and is clearly a prayer for divine guidance. The poem was entitled "The Pillar of Cloud," likening his pilgrimage to the Israelites' wilderness journey, with the phrase, "Lead Thou me on,"appearing five times — the essence of his prayer.

Lead on, O King eternal
Ernest W. Shurtleff, 1862-1917
Source: *Hymns of the Faith,* 1887
   For his graduation from Andover Theological Seminary in 1887, Shurtleff was asked by his classmates to write an appropriate hymn. Graduation is never an end — merely a road marker on the path of life. So the hymn is an appropriate call for us to be prepared to pitch our tents and to follow wherever God leads. The rousing marching tune by the self taught English organist and composer, Henry Smart, adds to the excitement of the call to march.

Lead us, heavenly Father, lead us
James Edmeston, 1791-1867
Source: *Sacred Lyrics,* 1821
   Edmeston, an architect, had what Percy Dearmer described as a "regrettable practice" of writing a hymn every Sunday evening to be read at family worship. Of the 2000 which he wrote, only one survives. The hymn is in the form of a Trinitarian prayer, addressing Father, Son and Holy Spirit.

Lead us, O Father, in the paths of peace
William H. Burleigh, 1812-1871
Source: *The New Congregational Hymn-Book,* 1859
   Although most hymns have been written by ministers, this was from the pen of a journalist, abolitionist, and harbor-master in New York City. In simple language, his hymn asks God's guidance in the paths of peace, truth, and right on the way to our heavenly rest.

Let all mortal flesh keep silence

Liturgy of St. James. Trans. Gerard Moultrie, 1829-1885
Source: *Lyra Eucharistica,* 1864

This ancient prayer at the opening of the Eucharist is one of the oldest liturgies of the Christian Church, traditionally ascribed to St. James, the brother of Jesus. Its first written form exists in the mid fourth century in both Greek and Syriac, and is still sung in Jerusalem on the Sunday after Christmas. It is appropriate for both communion services and the celebration of the Incarnation.

Let all the world in every corner sing

George Herbert, 1593-1633
Source: *The Temple,* 1633

John Wesley included six poems by Herbert in his first hymnal, published in Georgia in 1737. Herbert called this one "Antiphon" because of its refrain which is sung before and after each of the basic themes. Our songs *can reach* heaven; they *can grow* on earth. Stanza two refers to the law limiting church singing to psalms, but unless the heart is involved the singing will not reach its real potential. No excuses allowed — everybody sing!

Let all things now living

Katherine K. Davis, 1892-1980
Source: Anthem of the same title, 1939

Katherine Davis is well known for her many anthems, many of which used folk tunes, and for her collections of piano pieces, vocal duets, choral collections, cantatas, and operas. Many of her texts were written under various pseudonyms; she used "John Cowley" for this fine song of praise and thanksgiving. Long popular with choirs, it has recently been arranged for hymn usage in several new hymnals. The memorable Welsh tune THE ASH GROVE has played an important part in its popularity.

Let all together praise our God

Nikolaus Hermann, c. 1480-1561
Trans. Arthur Tozer Russell, 1806-1874
Source: *Die Sonntags-Evangelia,* 1560

German pastors have often been composers as well as poets, and Hermann's tune, with its charming rising scale to the last phrase, was written before the words to be sung to another of his hymns for children about the life of John the Baptist. He was an organist, a school teacher, choirmaster, and pupil and friend of Martin Luther. His hymn is an interesting explanation of the Incarnation, intended for children but equally valuable for adults.

Let saints on earth in concert sing
Charles Wesley, 1707-1788
Source: *Funeral Hymns,* 1759

The original first stanza of this hymn began, "Come, let us join our friends above" and was meant to be sung at a funeral as a statement about the Communion of Saints. Dr. J. E. Rattenbury commented about this hymn, "Death, it is true, like love, renders all distinctions void, but it cannot destroy the fellowship which love makes." Therefore Christians are all one family with some of us here and others having crossed the river of death to be with the living God.

Let the whole creation cry
Stopford August Brooke, 1832-1916
Source: *Christian Hymns* 1881

Psalm 148, with its call for everything in creation (the psalmist lists 30 things!), was the basis for this hymn by an Anglican clergyman who was appointed chaplain to the queen in 1867. It is one of few hymns which mention the arts as praising God.

Let us break bread together on our knees
Negro Spiritual
Source: *Negro Spirituals, Book II,* 1927

There are few spirituals which deal with communion, but the reverent simplicity and profound insights of this hymn have made it very popular in American hymnals since about 1955. The *Guide to the Pilgrim Hymnal* (1966) states, "The refrain reminds us of the publican's prayer, commended by Jesus (Luke 18:13), and of the age-old petition, 'Kyrie eleison' — Lord have mercy — which has been a part of the Communion Service in the Eastern Church since the fifth century, and of the Western Church since the sixth."

Let us with a gladsome mind
John Milton, 1608-1674
Source: *Poems of Mr. John Milton,* 1645

Milton was only a fifteen year old school boy at St. Paul's London, when he wrote 24 stanzas as a version of Psalm 136. The stanzas usually included in hymnals today deal only with nature. The refrain of the psalm, "for His mercy endureth forever," appears at the end of each stanza.

Lift high the cross, the love of Christ proclaim
George William Kitchin, 1827-1912. Revised Michael Robert
   Newbolt, 1874-1956

Source: *Hymns Ancient and Modern, Supplement,* 1916

This is a hymn which owes its popularity more to the tune CRUCIFER by Sydney H. Nicholson with its stirring refrain than to any great merit of the text — which is a revision of original lines by an Anglican who published works in the fields of history, biography and archaeology. It is related to "Onward, Christian Soldiers" and "For all the saints" in its symbolism of marching in the ranks of the soldiers of the crucified. It is the Crucified Christ and his cross which we follow, and his love we proclaim to the world.

Lift up your heads, ye mighty gates
Georg Weissel, 1590-1635
Trans. Catherine Winkworth, 1827-1878
Source: *Preussische Festlieder,* 1642

This is the most famous paraphrase of Psalm 24, and reveals a spirit of praise and hope unexpected from the depths of the dreadful years of the Thirty Years' War. Its theme is the preparation for the Messiah's coming, and is widely sung during the season of Advent.

Lo, He comes with clouds descending
Charles Wesley, 1707-1788
Source: *Hymns of Intercession for all Mankind,* 1758

Wesley used the first line but completely recast the rest of a crude hymn by John Cennick (author of the famous "Wesley" table grace, "Be present at our table, Lord"), six years after Cennick's death. The ideas and language are borrowed from the book of Revelation, and the whole is based on Rev. 1:7, "Behold, he cometh with clouds, and every eye shall see him, and they also which pierced him: and all kindreds of the earth shall wail because of him. Even so, Amen." The language is apocalyptic and should be interpreted symbolically, not literally.

Lo, how a rose e'er blooming
German anonymous. Trans. Theodore Baker, 1851-1934
Source: *Speirischen Gesangbuch,* 1599

This much translated Twelfth Night German hymn was current at the time of Luther and first appeared in a Cologne Catholic hymnal. It combines themes of the root of Jesse, the prophesy of Isaiah, the Virgin mother Mary, and Christ as the rose dispelling darkness and death. The traditional melody, with its subleties of rhythm, is usually sung to the famous harmonization by Michael Praetorius.

Look, ye saints! the sight is glorious
Thomas Kelly, 1769-1854

Source: *Hymns on Various Passages of Scriptures,* 1809

The theme is the "Second Advent," when Christ shall come in glory and judgment and "shall reign for ever and ever" (Revelation 11:15). The extravagant and apocalyptic language is a grand acclamation of the glory of that final day when Christ will be crowned "King of kings, and Lord of lords!" It is made even grander by the rousing Welsh hymn tune BRYN CALFARIA, with its fitting repetition of text.

Lord, Christ, when first Thou cam'st to men
Walter Russell Bowie, 1882-1969
Source: *Songs of Praise,* 1931

England was first to recognize the power of this text, which was written at the request of F. W. Dwelly, Dean of Liverpool Cathedral, who had asked for "a modern version of the *Dies Irae*" (day of wrath and judgment), "to express both the solemnity and inspiration of the thought of Christ coming into our modern world in judgment." It reminds us that every advent is both a first and second coming, and that Christ comes both in love and with judgment.

Lord, dismiss us with Thy blessing
John Fawcett, 1740-1817
Source: Supplement, *Shawbury Hymn Book,* 1773

Fawcett, best known for "Blest be the tie that binds," probably intended this hymn for the last Sunday of the year, asking God's blessing on the new year. However, it is generally sung at the conclusion of worship as a choral benediction. The author was an English Baptist minister who wrote over 160 hymns, mostly to be sung after his sermons.

Lord, I want to be a Christian
Negro Spiritual

In 1756 a slave in Hanover, VA went to the Presbyterian minister, William Davies, with the request: "I come to you, sir, that you may tell me some good things concerning Jesus Christ and my duty to God, for I am resolved not to live any more as I have done." This desire to be a Christian is a universal longing that is voiced in many spirituals — for patience, forbearance, love, faith and hope.

Lord Jesus Christ, be present now
Attr. Wilhelm II, 1598-1662
Trans. Catherine Winkworth, 1827-1878
Source: *Cantionale Sacrum,* 1651

Published anonymously in 1651, the text was not ascribed to Wilhelm II until 25 years later. During the Thirty Years' War the king was severely wounded, left for dead, and then taken a prisoner. Active in the Peace of Prague and the Peace of Westphalia, he later devoted his time to poetry and music. His hymn invites us to open our souls to Christ, to open our lips to praise, and to join with the angelic chorus in praising God.

Lord Jesus, think on me
Synesius of Cyrene, c.375-430
Trans. Allen W. Chatfield, 1808-1896
Source: *Hymns Ancient and Modern,* 1875

Of aristocratic family in North Africa, Synesius wrote nine hymns stating Christian doctrine in terms of neo-platonic philosophy. The hymn is a prayer for Jesus' help in all the times of need in this life and at the time of death. Benjamin Britten used this hymn in "Noye's Fludde" during the storm at sea when Noah feared that the ark would sink.

Lord, keep us steadfast in Thy word
Martin Luther, 1483-1546
Trans. Catherine Winkworth, 1827-1878
Source: *Magdeburg Geistliche Lieder,* 1542

When the Turkish army had overrun Hungary and was threatening Germany in 1541, Luther wrote and used this hymn in a special prayer service asking for God's protection. Original references to the Pope and the Turks were later omitted to make the hymn more generally useful. The Word of God was always uppermost in the mind of Luther, and we sing his prayer asking God to keep us faithful to the Word.

Lord of all being, throned afar
Oliver Wendell Holmes, 1809-1894
Source: *Atlantic Monthly,* 1859

Holmes included this hymn at the end of the last essay in the series *The Professor at the Breakfast Table.* God who created everything and lives in heaven, is near to everyone who lives a life of love. He is the light that brightens our lives, and the Lord of all life. The final stanza is based on the words of Jesus in John 8:32, "And ye shall know the truth, and the truth shall make you free." With a bit of punning, he called it a "Sun-day Hymn."

Lord of all hopefulness, Lord of all joy
Jan Struther, 1901-1953
Source: *Songs of Praise,* 1931

Using a pen name, Joyce Anstruther was a famous English teacher, poet, and novelist — her "Mrs. Miniver" was turned into a popular film. She wrote eleven hymns for the forward looking *Songs of Praise*, mostly in unusual meters and using contemporary style and language. Her hymns were among the first to address God with the pronoun "You." Frank Colquohoun in *A Hymn Companion* describes it as a hymn "with a human touch and a healthy spiritual tone."

Lord of our life, and God of our salvation
Philip Pusey, 1799-1855
Source: *Psalm and Hymn Tunes,* 1834

The hymn is a free paraphrase of Matthaus A. von Lowenstern's hymn, "Christe du beistand," written during the Thirty Years' War as a prayer for peace. Although written about the troubled state of the Church in England just before the Oxford Movement in the 1830's, it is a hymn for any troubled times, including our own. It is written in the unusual Sapphic Ode, with its three long lines of eleven syllables concluded by a short line of five.

Lord, speak to me that I may speak
Frances R. Havergal, 1836-1789
Source: *Under the Surface,* 1874

Based on Romans 14:7 ("None of us lives to himself, and no man dies to himself") and entitled "A Worker's Prayer," it is a fitting commentary on the life of the author whose delicate health forced her to conserve her energies and restrict her activities. It is a reminder that it is our duty to use the talents God gives us to share with others, praying that God will strengthen, teach, fill, and use us according to His will for our lives.

Lord, whose love through humble service
Albert F. Bayly, 1901-1984
Source: *Seven New Social Welfare Hymns,* 1961

The hymn was written in June, 1961 in response to an invitation by the Hymn Society of America to submit hymns on social welfare and was included in *Seven New Social Welfare Hymns.* As Christians we should follow the example of Christ, whose life was spent serving others. Our worship is church is vain unless it is followed by living concern for others.

Lord, who throughout these forty days
Claudia Frances Hernaman, 1838-1898
Source: *A Child's Book of Praise,* 1873

As a result of her life-long interest in religious education, the author wrote 150 hymns for children. This one attempts to explain the deeper meanings of the forty days of Lent — fasting, praying, temptations, penitence which point to the joys of Easter which follows the penitential season.

Love came down at Christmas
Christina G. Rossetti, 1830-1894
Source: *Time Flies,* 1885

The author, daughter of an Italian refugee who was professor of Italian at the University of London, because of her poor health turned her talents to intense religious devotion and writing many volumes of poetry and prose. Her hymns are exquisitely crafted with a minimum of words and with incisive and colorful imagery. The theme of "Love" made incarnate at Christmas has made this a popular hymn.

Love divine, all loves excelling
Charles Wesley, 1707-1788
Source: *Hymns for Those That Seek,* 1747

The idea for the hymn was taken from a popular song by the poet Dryden, "Fairest isle, all isles excelling." Its theme is the great thread of divine love which runs through all of Wesley's hymns. After a prayer addressed to Christ to dwell within our lives, the hymn turns to the theme of sanctification — God's "great salvation" is sufficient to deliver a Christian from the power as well as from the guilt of sin (2 Corinthians 5:17). Thus we are "going on to perfection," being "changed from glory into glory" (2 Corinthians 3:18).

Make me a captive, Lord
George Matheson, 1842-1906
Source: *Sacred Songs,* 1890

Entitled "Christian Freedom" and using the Ephesians 3:1 text, "Paul, the prisoner of Christ," the hymn is an excellent example of the use of parodox: captive-free, give up sword-conqueror be, imprison-strong, monarch throne-crown resign. The phrase "varies with the wind" refers to the amount of tension with which a spring is wound, not to the blowing of the wind. The author was a brilliant student and preacher, but suffered poor eyesight, being virtually blind by his 18th birthday.

May the grace of Christ our Savior
John Newton, 1724-1807
Source: *Olney Hymns,* 1779

This is a metrical paraphrase of 2 Corinthians 3:14 ("The grace of the Lord Jesus Christ, and the love of God, and the communion of the Holy Spirit be with you all'') which is followed by the promise that if we have these blessings and abide with each other in love, our joys will be those of heaven itself.

Mine eyes have seen the glory of the coming of the Lord
Julia Ward Howe, 1819-1910
Source: *Atlantic Monthly,* 1862

The patriotic folk song, "John Brown's Body," was an abolitionist battle hymn; but J. Freeman Clarke suggested that Mrs. Howe should write some new words for the tune. Awaking early in a Washington, DC hotel in the pre-dawn, the words came to her in a rush of inspiration. It is one of the most powerful of all calls for a nation to purge itself under the judgment of God and to march to the beat of the drums of God.

More love to Thee, O Christ
Elizabeth P. Prentiss, 1818-1878
Source: *Songs of Devotion for Christian Associations,* 1870

The author, in early life a school teacher and later the wife of the professor of homiletics at Union Theological Seminary in New York City, has only one theme: let me love Christ more than earthly pleasures, peace or rest, and in spite of sorrow, grief, pain, or even death.

Morning has broken
Eleanor Farjeon, 1881-1965
Source: *Songs of Praise,* 1931

Sometimes the secular world helps make a sacred song popular, and this is the case with this hymn. The Gaelic melody first appeared with a Christmas text, "Child in a manger," but was the source of inspiration for the morning text by Eleanor Farjeon, who wrote nursery rhymns and singing games for children. How marvelous it is to think that the dawn of each new day is just as fresh and full of opportunities as was the first day of creation. God is always giving us another chance!

My country, 'tis of thee
Samuel F. Smith, 1808-1895
Source: *Union Collection of Church Music,* 1832

The famous early American church musician, Lowell Mason, was given some books from Germany which he turned over to a young theological student at Andover Seminary with the suggestion that he might translate some of them or write some new words if he saw an attractive tune. The result was one of our finest patriotic hymns set to the tune of the British national hymn, "God save the King." It combines patriotic fervor with a prayer that God will bless and protect us in liberty and freedom.

My faith looks up to Thee
Ray Palmer, 1808-1887
Source: *Spiritual Songs for Social Worship,* 1831
Dr. Ray Palmer, one of America's most distinguished Congregationalist ministers, wrote his most famous hymn at the age of 22, shortly after he graduated from Yale in 1830. In Boston he met Lowell Mason, who was compiling a new hymn book, who asked for some contributions. Struck by the simplicity and sincerity of the expression of faith, Mason composed the tune OLIVET to which it has always been sung.

My God, I love Thee; not because I hope for heaven thereby
St. Francis Xavier, 1506-1552
Trans. Edward Caswall, 1814-1878
Source: *Epitome de la vida y muerte de San Ignacio de Loyola,* 1662
In sonnet form (a rhyme scheme of abba cddc eee eee in fourteen lines) the Spanish poem is an exploration of motives for loving God. We must not love for selfish reasons (to acquire merit, gain heaven, or for fear of eternal death) but simply because of what God has done for us. "We love Him, because He first loved us" is the simple message.

My hope is built on nothing less
Edward Mote, 1797-1874
Source: *Hymns of Praise, A New Selection of Gospel Hymns,* 1836
Entitled "The Immutable Basis of a Sinner's Hope," the hymn began in Mote's mind with the refrain, "On Christ the solid rock I stand, All other ground is sinking sand," combining many New Testament references. The author began as a cabinet maker and was quite irreligious. He wrote, "O ignorant was I that I did not know there was a God." Converted, he became an English Baptist pastor, and his hymn is thoroughly evangelical in its message of personal trust and faith in Jesus Christ.

My Shepherd will supply my need
Isaac Watts, 1674-1748
Source: *Psalms of David,* 1719

No psalm has inspired more hymn settings than the 23rd, and Watt's development of the theme of the house of heaven with an inspired conclusion is not found in the psalm itself: "No more a stranger, or a guest, but like a child at home." The text was raised from long neglect by its setting to the famous tune RESIGNATION from the 1835 *Southern Harmony* — a collection of folk hymns collected in the southern Appalachian mountains.

My song is love unknown
Samuel Crossman, 1624-1684
Source: *The Young Man's Meditation,* 1664
Crossman was one of the small group of 17th century writers whose sacred poems have become part of our heritage. Written when only psalm singing was permissible, it moved to a more personal expression of emotions. Beginning with the Incarnation, it moves directly to the events of Holy Week. The Savior's love is defined by his life and death and the writer defines our response in continual praise.

Nature with open volume stands
Isaac Watts, 1674-1748
Source: *Hymns and Spiritual Songs,* 1707
How can we best see and understand God? Watts, reminding us of Romans 1:20, "The invisible things of God from the creation of the world are clearly seen, being understood by the things that are made," describes nature as an open book where we can see God. But it is in the work of redemption through Christ on the cross that we see God's power, wisdom, and love. Thus the original title was "The Wonders of the Cross."

Near the cross her vigil keeping
Jacopone da Todi, 1230-1306
Trans. Louis F. Benson, 1855-1930
Source: *Roman Missal,* 1727
(See "At the cross her station keeping.")

Nearer my God to Thee
Sarah F. Adams, 1805-1848
Source: *Hymns and Anthems,* 1841
Mrs. Adams submitted thirteen texts for a Unitarian collection. Her most famous one is based on the story of Jacob's dream at Bethel (Genesis 28:11-19). Jacob had sinned, wronged his brother and was a fugitive from God. But God in Jacob's dream revealed divine mercy and promised that He would always be near to guide. The result is a text which should be sung exuberantly — it is not a funeral hymn!

New every morning is the love
John Keble, 1792-1866
Source: *The Christian Year*, 1827

Keble, like Thomas Ken a century earlier, wrote a hymn for both morning and evening. (Keble's evening hymn is the well known "Sun of my soul.") Based on Lamentations 3:22,23 ("His compassions fail not; they are new every morning") it has two basic themes: if we face each day with God it will take on new meanings and hallow our thoughts; we serve God not only in religious activities but in the commonplace things of life.

New songs of celebration
Erik Routley, 1917-1982
Source: *Cantate Domino*, 1975

Frank Colquhoun in *A Hymn Companion* 1985 says, "Erik Routley's encyclopedic knowledge of hymnody in all its varied aspects — historical, musical, liturgical, theological — made him the acknowledged authority on the subject throughout the world." This hymn is a paraphrase of Psalm 98 ("Sing to the Lord a new song"), and was written to provide an exhuberant paean of praise to match the marvelous tune for the psalm in the Genevan Psalter. It is a joyous celebration of God as creator, sovereign and judge of all the world.

Not alone for mighty empire
William P. Merrill, 1867-1954
Source: *Continent*, 1911

Brick Presbyterian Church in New York City was pastored between 1883 and 1938 by three famous hymn writers: Henry Van Dyke, Maltbie D. Babcock, and William P. Merrill. While Merrill was a pastor in Chicago in 1909 he was moved by a Thanksgiving Day sermon to write a prayer that God will save us from becoming divided by race, creed, class and faction — a prayer that is still needed today.

Now thank we all our God
Martin Rinkart, 1586-1649
Trans. Catherine Winkworth, 1827-1878
Source: *Praxis Pietatis Melica*, 1647

During the darkest days of the Thirty Years' War, Lutheran Pastor Rinkart could still write a table grace expressing thanks for God's gifts in the past, praying for guidance for the future, and ending with a majestic outburst of worship and praise to the Triune God.

Now the day is over
Sabine Baring-Gould, 1834-1924
Source: *Church Times,* 1867
   Proverbs 3:24 ("When you lie down, you shall not be afraid: yea, you shall lie down, and your sleep shall be sweet".) Was the inspiration for this eight stanza hymn which was once a most popular closing hymn for Sunday evening hymn sings around the campfire.

Now the green blade riseth
John Macleod Campbell Crum, 1872
Source: *Oxford Book of Carols,* 1928
   At the request of the editors of the famous *Oxford Book of Carols,* Crum wrote an Easter text to be sung to the French Christmas carol tune, NOEL NOUVELET. Its theme is the unquenchable and unkillable nature of love. Just as wheat dies in the ground, it rises to new life just as Christ was slain but rose from the grave. Springtime thus becomes a symbol of the Easter story.

Now the silence
Jaroslav J. Vajda, b. 1919
Source: *This Day,* May 1968
   Just as Gilbert and Sullivan built their reputation as a team for writing operettas, Jaroslav Vajda and Carl Schalk are building theirs as writers and composers of fine new hymns. The author has written, ". . .the hymn began to form in my mind as a list of awesome and exciting things that one should expect in worship, culminating in the Eucharist and benediction. The introit or entrance hymn resulted." It originally appeared without any punctuation (immediately capturing one's attention); there is no rhyme, no worn cliche, only rhythm and repetition to make it singable. Again the author, "The reversal of the Trinitarian order in the benediction was made not only to make the conclusion memorable, but to indicate the order in which the Trinity approaches us in worship: The Spirit brings us the gospel, by which God's blessing is released in our lives."

O be joyful in the Lord
Curtis Beach, b. 1914
Source: *Pilgrim Hymnal,* 1958
   When new hymnals are published, many new texts are submitted for consideration, but relatively few are chosen. Beach, a Congregational minister in California and Pennsylvania, had two of his submissions included in the *Pilgrim Hymnal,* both psalm paraphrases. Based on Psalm 100, this was written in the unusual meter of the traditional Hebrew melody, ROCK OF AGES (MOOZ

TSUR) and is worthy of comparison with the more famous settings of Kethe and Watts.

O beautiful for spacious skies
Katharine Lee Bates, 1859-1929
Source: *The Congregationalist,* 1895

Sometimes a hymn is born in a moment of inspiration and never changed, but Miss Bates' original poem, written after climbing Pikes Peak and gazing across the plains to the east, was altered twice by her — in 1904 and finally in 1918. The "alabaster cities" of stanza three refers to the "White City" of the Columbian World Exposition at Chicago which she visited on the way to Colorado. Its patriotic fervor has made the hymn a "second" national anthem.

O bread of life from heaven
Anon. Latin, c. 1661
Source: *Mainz Gesangbuch,* 1661. Trans. Composite

The hymn, probably by a 17th century German Jesuit, has been translated by at least six different poets, but all follow the basic two themes: Christ's body and blood as expressed in "O Bread" and "O Fount." The last stanza expresses our thanks for these means of grace, and our hopes to behold Christ face to face at the last Great Supper.

O Christ, the healer, we have come
Fred Pratt Green, b. 1903
Source: *Hymns and Songs,* 1969

"Are people writing hymns today?" is a question often asked by worshipers. The answer is a strong affirmative! This hymn by the English Methodist minister was written to fill the need for a text on health and wholeness. Green is considered to be one of the major text writers of all time and certainly one who stands as the most significant hymn writer today.

O come, all ye faithful
Anonymous Latin, 18th Century
Trans. Frederick Oakeley, 1802-1880
Source: *Murray's Hymnal,* 1852

John Francis Wade, an Englishman who made his living by copying plainchant and other music, was the probably author as well as composer of this hymn. In spite of irregular scansion and lack of any rhyming the hymn is perhaps the most popular Christmas hymn (as distinguished from carols).

O come, O come Emmanuel (Immanuel)
Latin, 12th Century. Trans. John M. Neale, 1818-1866 and
   Henry S. Coffin, 1877-1954
Source: *Psalteriolum Cantionum Catholicarum,* 1710
   From the seven antiphons sung in the medieval Roman Church
at Vespers before and after the *Magnificat* (Mary's Song), just prior
to Christmas, sometime in the 13th century five were selected for
a hymn and the "Rejoice, rejoice" refrain added. Biblical references
to the Great "O's" are: Emmanuel (Isaiah 7:14), Root of Jesse (Isaiah
11:10), Dayspring (Malachi 4:2), Key of David (Isaiah 22:22), and
O Lord (Adonai) (Exodus 3:15). The purpose of Advent is to prepare for Christmas, as Lent prepares for Easter.

O Day of God, draw nigh
Robert Balgarnie Young Scott, b. 1899
Source: *Leaflet of Fellowship for a Christian Social Order,* 1937
   The hymn by the United Church of Canada minister who was
Professor of Religion at Princeton University 1955-1968 was based
on Zephaniah 1:14-18 and is a call for social reform. The "Day of
God" is that spoken of by the prophet Isaiah in chapters 24-27, a
day of judgment but also a day of salvation. The biblical order of
justice first and peace next is a reminder that peace is the fruit of
righteousness (Isaiah 32:17).

O day of rest and gladnesss
Christopher Wordsworth, 1807-1885
Source: *The Holy Year,* 1862
   "Remember the Sabbath day to keep it holy" is one of the com-
mandments. The nephew of the famous William Wordsworth wrote
his hymn to remind us that we still should make it a day of rest, of
glad worship, and joyful reminder of Christ's resurrection. Every
Sunday celebrates Easter day!

O dearest Lord, Thy sacred Head
Henry Ernest Hardy, 1869-1946
Source: *The Divine Compassion,*
   Hardy, known as Brother Andrew of the Order of the Divine Compassion, was born in India, but lived most of his life in England.
A deeply personal devotional hymn, it is reminiscent of such medieval
hymns as "O Sacred Head now wounded" in its references to the
head, hands, feet and heart of Jesus "pierced for me." Our response?
— to think, work, follow and live for Christ.

O for a closer walk with God
William Cowper, 1731-1800
Source: *Olney Hymns,* 1779
Imagine what it would be like to walk with God! In Genesis 5:24 we read that "Enoch walked with God: and he was not; for God took him." Deeply anxious for a very ill friend, Cowper wrote the hymn in an endeavor "to surrender to the Lord" his "dearest comforts." If we can let go of our concerns, hate our sins, and throw down our idols we can face life or death with calmness and serenety.

O for a heart to praise my God
Charles Wesley, 1707-1788
Source: *Hymns and Sacred Poems,* 1740
On the Anniversary Day of his conversion, Wesley wrote an 18 stanza hymn. Even John thought this too long and and reduced it for his hymnal. The Moravian Peter Böhler's comment to Charles, "If I had a thousand tongues, I would praise Christ with them all" was the trigger for a hymn of deep personal experience and also a profound sense of evangelical concern for the world.

O gladsome light, O grace
Greek Hymn, 2nd Century
Trans. Robert S. Bridges, 1844-1930
Source: *Yattendon Hymnal,* 1899
It is believed that this early church hymn for lamplighting goes as far back as the days of the catacombs, when light in darkness had special significance. Although most hymns were addressed to God, this was addressed to Christ who is the gladdening and holy Light, the glory of God, and the giver of life.

O God of Bethel, by whose hand
Philip Doddridge, 1702-1751, as revised in *Scottish Paraphrases,* 1781
Source: *Hymns,* post. 1755
Modern day lack of knowledge of the Scriptures makes hymns such as this obscure to many worshipers. The hymn, headed "Jacob's Vow; from Genesis 28:20-22" is a paraphrase of the story of Jacob making a vow with God at Bethel: "If God will be with me, and will keep me in this way that I go, and will give me bread to eat, and raiment to put on, so that I come again to my father's house in peace; then shall the Lord be my God." The revision in the *Scottish Paraphrases* brings us all personally into the story and into a covenant with God.

O God of earth and altar
Gilbert K. Chesterton, 1874-1936
Source: *The Commonwealth*, 1906
Would you expect an author of detective stories to write a hymn? In addition to writing in the fields of theology, history, criticism and biography Chesterton also wrote the famous "Father Brown" detective stories. His hymn is a strong plea that the government, the church and the people repent of evil and united become a force for good in the world.

O God of every nation
William W. Reid, Jr., b. 1923
Source: *Twelve New Order Hymns*, 1958
This hymn won first place in a national hymn-writing contest of the Hymn Society of America in cooperation with the Department of International Affairs of the National Council of Churches. It is a powerful hymn of "social concern" and ι prayer to end those things which divide and destroy us. A Methodist minister, he, like his father who was the editor of *The Hymn*, has been active in the Hymn Society and has published several hymns.

O God of light, Thy Word, a lamp unfailing
Sarah E. Taylor, 1883-1954
Source: *Ten New Hymns on the Bible*, 1952
The Hymn Society of America sponsored a search for new hymns on the Bible to celebrate the publication of the Revised Standard Version of the Bible in 1952, and Miss Taylor's winning hymn was sung by two million people in thousands of communities. Starting with the simple idea of Psalm 119:105 ("Thy word is a lamp unto my feet, and a light unto my path") she has provided a fine historical perspective of how the Bible came to be written, and what it has to offer to the world.

O God of love, O King of peace
Henry W. Baker, 1821-1877
Source: *Hymns Ancient and Modern*, 1861
The famous chairman of the most famous hymnal of all times, *Hymns Ancient and Modern*, wrote this hymn especially for that book, with the heading "The Lord shall give his people the blessing of peace" — the theme is found throughout the scriptures. It is a prayer that God give us peace and that we turn from our foolish ways of war.

O God, Thou faithful God (O God, eternal source)
Johann Heermann, 1585-1647

Trans. Catherine Winkworth, 1827-1878
Source: *Devoti musica cordis*, 1630
Entitled "A daily prayer," the hymn was written during the time of Heermann's greatest suffering. During the Thirty Years' War he lost all his possessions, narrowly escaped death, his town was plundered and devasted by fire and plague. His hymn faces all this with three fundamental principles: holy living, patience in tribulation and joy in death.

O God, whose will is life and good (originally: Father, whose will . . .)
Hardwicke D. Rawnsley, 1851-1920
Source: *A Missionary Hymn Book*, 1922
One of the important works of missionaries has been in the field of medicine, carrying the love of God through restoring health and improving the quality of life. This hymn is one of very few which offers a prayer to strengthen the hand of physicians and all those who care for the sick.

O holy city, seen of John
Walter Russell Bowie, 1882-1969
Source: *Hymns of the Kingdom of God*, 1910
Often the holy city described in Revelation is so far off that it seems unreal. President Henry Sloane Coffin asked Dr. Bowie of the faculty at Union Theological Seminary in New York City to write "some new hymns that would express the convictions that our hope of the Kingdom of God is not alone some far-off eschatological possibility but in the beginnings, at least, may be prepared for here on our actual earth."

O Holy Spirit, by whose breath
Latin, 9th Century. Trans. John Webster Grant, b. 1919
Source: *Canadian Hymn Book*, 1971
This is a contemporary translation of the famous "Veni Creator" (Come Holy Ghost). The distinguished Canadian theologian says, "My hymns are, without exception, translations. . .but what I have done in each case is to try to envisage the meaning of the words for the 20th century and to reproduce it as well as I could. At various times I have been seized with the conviction that a particular set of words needed to be given an updated English version." The author succeeded!

Oh how shall I receive Thee (O Lord, how shall I meet you)
Paul Gerhardt, 1607-1676

Trans. Catherine Winkworth, 1827-1878
Source: *D. M. Luthers und anderer vornehmen geistreichen,*
1653

How do we prepare to meet Christ? We might bring palms as people did long ago, but better still we can bring our love which reflects Christ's love that led him to be born, to serve humanity and to give us his life for us. What a fitting hymn to sing during the Advent season!

O Jesus Christ, may grateful hymns be rising
Bradford G. Webster, 1898-
Source: *Five New Hymns on the City,* 1954

For many years the Hymn Society of America has been a leader in the encouragement of writing new texts on pertinent themes for which few hymns have been written. Webster's hymn was written to express the deep concerns modern urban society finds in our cities. He is a retired Methodist minister, having served New York state churches for forty years.

O Jesus, I have promised
John Ernest Bode, 1816-1874
Source: *SPCK leaflet,* 1868

Based on Luke 9:57, "Lord, I will follow thee whithersoever thou goest," the hymn was written by the author for the confirmation of his three children. But it says much more and is a prayer for Christ's presence at all times — in the struggle against sin, in the midst of the world's temptations, and the struggles with the "storms of passion." Jesus has promised us to be with him in glory, but we must also promise to follow and serve him to the end.

O Jesus, Thou art standing
William Walsham How, 1823-1897
Source: Supplement to *Psalms and Hymns,* 1867

"Behold, I stand at the door and knock" is found at Revelation 3:20, and this passage was the inspiration of both this hymn and the famous painting by Holman Hunt, "The Light of the World," which shows Christ knocking at the door waiting for us to let him in to our lives. Jesus may stand, knocking and pleading, but He can only enter if we open the door.

O little town of Bethlehem
Phillips Brooks, 1835-1893
Source: *The Church Porch,* 1874

The famous preacher (first in Philadelphia where this hymn was written, and later at Trinity Church, Boston) returned from a pilgrimage to the Holy Land where he had found himself on Christmas Eve at the field of the Shepherds. Wishing to share his impressions and feelings in hymn form, he wrote the words for the children of his church and the Sunday School superintendent jotted down a tune and a hymn was first sung on December 27, 1868. The story begins with Christ born in Bethlehem; it ends with Christ born in the heart.

O Lord my God! When I in awesome wonder
(See: "How Great Thou Art")

O love, how deep, how broad, how high
Attr. to Thomas à. Kempis, 1379-1471.
Trans. Benjamin Webb, 1819-1885
Source: *Karlsruhe ms.,* 15th Century
   Is it really possible to measure the dimensions of the love of God — how deep, how broad, how high? This ancient hymn attempts to do it by rehearsing the entire life, ministry, death, resurrection and ascension of Christ plus the sending of the Holy Spirit. And all of Christ's life and work was "for us" — a phrase which is repeated over and over.

O love of God, how strong and true
Horatio Bonar, 1809-1889
Source: *Hymns of Faith and Hope,* 1861
   The love of God lies at the heart of the Christian message, and that love is not an abstract idea but an act of redemption. William Temple points out that the essence of Christianity is not "God is love" but "God so loved that he gave," and this love is the theme of the great Scottish writer's hymn.

O love that casts out fear
Horatio Bonar, 1808-1889
Source: *Hymns of Faith and Hope,* 1861
   Bonar is not a name that is very familiar to hymn singers, yet over 100 of his hymns have been included in various hymnals — the most famous being his communion hymn, "Here, O my Lord, I see Thee face to face." Yet his easy flow of ideas in this hymn is the mark of a fine poet. God's love is seen as casting out fear and sin, as sunlight of the soul, and the well-spring of heavenly peace.

O love that wilt not let me go
George Matheson, 1842-1906

Source: *Life and Work,* January 1882

Sometimes great hymns are written very quickly in moments of brilliant insight. Such was the case with both words and tune. Matheson says, "It was written with extreme rapidity; it seemed to me that its compositon occupied only a few minutes." And the composer of ST. MARGARET, Dr. Albert L. Peace, said, "After reading it very carefully, I wrote the tune straight off, and may say that the ink of the first note was hardly dry when I had finished the tune." The text deals with Love, Light, Joy, and the Cross — all giving reassurance in times of sorrow.

O Master, let me walk with Thee

Washington Gladden, 1836-1918
Source: *Sunday Afternoon,* 1879

Gladden, one of America's best known Congregationalist ministers, was a powerful and fearless advocate of the "social gospel." The heart of his message is found in the first two lines, "O Master, let me walk with Thee, In lowly paths of service free" and the poem was entitled "Walking with God."

O my soul, bless God the Father

Anon. version of Psalm 103
Source: *United Presbyterian Book of Psalms,* 1871

Originally in sixteen stanzas, the metrical version of Psalm 103 is remarkably faithful to the original, which can be ascertained by comparing the two verse by verse. The psalm is a catalogue of reasons why we should bless God and forget not all his mercies to proclaim.

O perfect Love, all human thoughts transcending

Dorothy B.. Gurney, 1858-1932
Source: *Hymns Ancient and Modern,* 1889

This is probably the most popular of all wedding hymns. It was written by Mrs. Gurney for her sister's marriage. The first tune used was by John B. Dykes, but Joseph Barnby's setting written for a royal wedding in 1889 made the new tune the perennial favorite.

O sacred Head now wounded (sore wounded) (surrounded)

Anon. Latin. Trans. to German, Paul Gerhardt, 1607-1676
    Trans. to English, James W. Alexander, 1804-1859
Source: *Praxis Pietatis Melica,* 1656

The original Latin poem addressed seven Aspects of the Crucified: feet, knees, hands, side, breast, heart and face. Known as "crucifix hymns" they were designed for long, intense devotions while kneeling at the altar. Part seven, *salve caput,* was put into German by the famous hymn writer, Paul Gerhardt. An American Presbyterian minister and seminary professor translated it into English, and it was first published in *The Christian Lyre,* 1830 — an early American hymnal with many folk tunes. Thus we have a hymn which has survived two different translations and still retains the intensity of the original Latin.

O sing a song of Bethlehem
Louis F. Benson, 1855-1930
Source: *School Hymnal,* 1899
   Benson, America's premier hymnologist, left his library of 8000 volumes to Princeton Seminary. He also edited four hymnals, writing this particular hymn for children and youth as a teaching hymn about the life of Christ. It is built around four places: Bethlehem, Nazarath, Galilee, and Calvary — ending with the resurrection.

O sons and daughters, let us sing
Jean Tisserand, d. 1494. Trans. John Mason Neale, 1818-1866
Source: Untitled book, published between 1518 and 1536
   This is an Easter carol in narrative style. Yes, there are carols for other seasons than Christmas! After an opening call to praise, we are reminded of the women coming to the tomb, the angels' message to them, Christ appearing to the disciples at the evening, and even the story of doubting Thomas. The tune, although in minor, has the joyous quality of a dance tune.

O Spirit of the living God
James Montgomery, 1771-1854
Source: *Evangelical Magazine,* August 1823
   Written for a missionary rally in 1823, the hymn "takes the highest place for good doctrine, literary skill and general grace" according to the hymnologist, Erik Routley. The church in every generation needs to pray for a fresh outpouring of the Holy Spirit to fill it with love and power to "preach the reconciling word" throughout the world.

O splendor of God's glory bright
Ambrose of Milan, 340-397
Trans. Robert S. Bridges, 1844-1930
Source: Medieval manuscript
   Ambrose can be called the father of modern hymnody, for it was he who began the use of meter in hymns, with Long Meter (four lines of poetry, each with eight syllables) predominant. The use of

"light" (five times in stanza one) helps to remind us of God's splendor
— which is indescribable.

O that I had a thousand voices
Johann Mentzer, 1658-1734
Trans. Catherine Winkworth, 1827-1878
Source: *Neues Geistreiches Gesangbuch,* 1704

Do you really use the one tongue and voice you have to adequately praise God? The author, who was a friend of Zinzendorf, whose estate was turned over to the singing refugee Moravians, was so filled with praise that he wished for a thousand tongues better to honor God. The translator, an English lady active in educational and social work, was the finest translator of German hymns, with most hymnals including 15 to 20 from her three books.

O what their joy and their glory must be
Peter Abelard, 1079-1142
Trans. John Mason Neale, 1818-1866
Source: St. Gall manuscript, 13th Century

This is one of the hymns from Abelard's complete hymnal written for Abbess Heloise and the convent near Nogent-sur-Seine. It is a joyful celebration of the life of heaven, and was written to be sung Saturday evenings as preparation for Sunday, the Christian Sabbath.

O where are kings and empires now
Arthur Cleveland Coxe, 1818-1896
Source: *Churchman,* 1839

When the author was a seminary student he wrote a ballad called "Chelsea" which began with the unlikely hymnic line. "When old Canute the Dane was merry England's King." After it was quoted by President Woolsey of Yale University in an address in New York City, an English hymnal editor selected stanzas which could make it into a hymn. Although the author served on the hymnal committee for the Episcopal church, he refused to allow his hymn to be included. Now, no hymnal would dare to omit it.

O Word of God incarnate
William W. How, 1823-1897
Source: *Supplement* to *Psalms and Hymns,* 1867

The author, known as the "poor man's bishop" in East London, wrote this hymn based on Psalm 119:105 ("Thy word is a lamp unto my feet, and a light unto my path") but headed it with Proverbs 6:23 ("For the commandment is a lamp; and the law is light; and reproofs of instruction are the way of life"). It develops many pictures of

God's Word, but the word "incarnate" strongly indicates that it is also about Christ as the living Word.

O worship the King
Robert Grant, 1779-1838
Source: *Church Psalmody,* 1833
   Grant, of Scottish birth, became a member of Parliament, Judge Advocate General, and was knighted when appointed Governor of Bombay. His hymn is in the same unusual meter as William Kethe's version and is a free paraphrase of Psalm 104, which celebrates in rich language the works of God in creation. The last two stanzas are more personal in character, with the last (often omitted, unfortunately) beginning "O measureless Might, ineffable Love."

O Zion, haste, thy mission high fulfilling
Mary Ann Thomson, 1834-1923
Source: *Church Hymns,* 1894
   While one of her children was ill with typhoid fever, Mrs. Thomson started writing her hymn with a tune in mind — but she wasn't satisfied with the chorus and didn't finish the hymn until three years later. Born in London, she married the librarian of the Free Library in Philadelphia, writing much religious poetry. The theme is "missions," with a call to "publish the glad tidings" to the world.

Of the Father's love begotten
Aurelius Clemens Prudentius, 348-c. 413
Trans. John M. Neale, 1818-1866, and
   Henry W. Baker, 1821-1877
Source: *Cathemerinon,* 4th Century
   87.87.87. is a popular meter in all hymnals, and probably was invented by Prudentius, who became a Christian at age 57 after serving as a judge and chief of the Imperial Guard to Emperor Honorius. The hymn was No. 9 in a collection of 12 hymns for the daily hours (offices). It was the author's interest that every hour of the day the believer should be reminded of Christ as the Alpha and the Omega, the beginning and the end.

On Jordan's bank the Baptist's cry
Charles Coffin, 1676-1749. Trans. John Chandler, 1806-1878
Source: *Paris Breviary,* 1736
   When Chandler translated the hymn from Latin he thought that it was a medieval work, but it was by a distinguished French scholar of the 18th century who wrote more than 100 hymns in Latin. Its theme is John the Baptist's announcement of Christ's advent and his

call to the people of Israel to repent and prepare for His coming.

On this day, the first of days
Latin: *Die parente temporum*
Trans. Henry W. Baker, 1821-1877
Source: *Le Mans Breviary,* 1748

This hymn is a reminder of why we worship on Sunday. While God created the earth and rested on the seventh day, it was on the "first day of the week" (in the Jewish calendar) that Christ rose from the dead. So every Sunday becomes for Christians a day to celebrate Easter and the resurrection, and stanza three is a reminder of Christ's central role. The rest of the hymn is addressed to the Trinity, asking for light and grace from the Holy Spirit, and praying that God's will be done.

Once in royal David's city
Cecil Frances Alexander, 1818-1895
Source: *Hymns for Little Children,* 1848

Mrs. Alexander, wife of an Irish Anglican bishop, heard some of her godchildren complaining about the dreariness of the Catechism. So she set to writing hymns (poems) which would explain the various phrases in more interesting style. This is based on the clause in the Creed, "who was conceived of the Holy Ghost, born of the Virgin Mary." Its popularity has been enhanced by Henry Gauntlett's tune and the superb recording of the Festival of Lessons and Carols from King's College Chapel, Cambridge, with a small boy singing stanza one with no accompaniment as the choir begins its processional.

Once to every man and nation
James Russell Lowell, 1819-1891
Source: *"The Present Crisis,"* in *Poems,* 1849

Lowell's poem was written as a protest against the Mexican War and the possibility of annexing the new Southwest Territory, enlarging the area of slaveholding states. It owes its appearance in hymnals to the work of an English hymnodist who selected 32 lines, rearranged them, and made some alterations. The text is not for squeamish Christians, for it calls for facing up to difficult decisions. The Welsh tune EBENEZER has the right mood and flavor to match the words.

Onward, Christian soldiers
Sabine Baring-Gould, 1834-1924
Source: *Church Times,* October 15, 1864

When the author became curate-in-charge of the mission church at Horbury Bridge, he needed a marching hymn for the Whit-Monday procession when the Sunday school children marched to a neighboring village for a festival. "I wanted the children to sing when marching," he wrote, "but couldn't think of anything quite suitable, so I sat up at night, resolved to write something myself." The children followed a processional cross, and the various "military" references were never meant to be construed as war-like or militaristic. Stanza three is one of the great stanzas about the church.

Open now thy gates of beauty
Benjamin Schmolck, 1672-1737
Trans. Catherine Winkworth, 1827-1878
Source: *Kirchen-Gefährte,* 1732
The hymn, entitled "Appearing before God," is only one of more than 1000 hymns written by the Lutheran pastor in predominantly Catholic Schweidnitz, where he was severely restricted in his work. He was a popular preacher, and despite poor health and eyesight carried on a vigorous and successful ministry, aided in part by his fine hymns.

Our Father, by whose name
F. Bland Tucker, 1895-1984
Source: *The Hymnal,* 1940
This hymn for families was written in 1939 in 66.66.88. meter, but was revised to fit the meter of the Welsh tune RHOSYMEDRE (Lovely) for the new Episcopal hymnal. Many hymns are paraphrases of or are based upon scripture. Stanza two of this hymn is based on Luke 2:52 ("And Jesus increased in wisdom and in stature, and in favor with God and man"). It is one of the few excellent hymns about family life and responsibility.

Our God our help in ages past (O God....alt.
John Wesley, 1703-1791)
Isaac Watts, 1674-1748
Source: *Psalms of David, Imitated in the Language of the New*
  Testament, 1719
The hymn is a paraphrase of verses 1-11 of Psalm 90. It was written in the form of Hebrew poetry: Thesis stated in st. 1-4 (God's goodness and providence); Antithesis stated in st. 5 (Our mortality); Synthesis in st. 6 (God continues to demonstrate care and protection and will be our eternal home). John Wesley changed the first word to "O", feeling that it reached out to everyone and was more inclusive.

Out of the depths I cry to Thee
Martin Luther, 1483-1546
Trans. Catherine Winkworth, 1827-1878
Source: *Etlich Christliche Lieder,* 1524 *and Enchiridion,* 1524
   In addition to his famous versions for the "German Mass," Luther is famous for his psalm paraphrases. Based on Psalm 130 it was sung to Luther's own tune by him in a time of great anxiety when confined in the castle of Coburg. He told his servant, "Come, let us defy the devil, and praise God by singing the hymn 'Aus tiefer Not schrei ich zu dir'." It was sung again in Halle when Luther died. The powerful text is matched by the tune in austere Phrygian mode.

Praise and thanksgiving
Albert F. Bayly, 1901-1984
Source: *Again, I Say, Rejoice,* 1967
   This text was written for the old Gaelic melody BUNESSAN, usually sung to "Morning has broken." Bayly wrote about this hymn, "This was written to meet the need for harvest thanksgiving hymns which remind us that we can thank God for his gifts rightly only if we are ready to do His will by sharing those gifts with others, so they can rejoice with us." It begins with praise to God for good gifts, turns to prayer for those who make harvest possible, and ends with sharing with one another.

Praise God from whom all blessings flow
Thomas Ken, 1637-1711
Source: *Manual of Prayers,* 1695
   The famous Doxology is often used at the Offertory in American churches, but is actually the final stanza of the three hymns which Bishop Ken wrote for personal devotions of the boys at Winchester College (singing only in their rooms). There were hymns for Morning, Evening, and Midnight. When sung to the OLD HUNDREDTH tune (from the Genevan Psalter) in the original rhythm, the word "Praise" rings out as a clarion call for all to join in praising the Triune God.

Praise, my soul, the King of heaven
Henry F. Lyte, 1793-1847
Source: *Spirit of the Psalms,* 1834
   While earlier hymnodists made paraphrases of hymns, Lyte, who won the prize for poetry three years in a row at Trinity College, Dublin, added a new dimension by making them poetical interpretations. This version of Psalm 103 includes such memorable lines as "Ransomed, healed, restored, forgiven," and "Father-like he tends

and spares us." Unfortunately a stanza based on verses 15-17 beginning "Frail as summer's flower we flourish, Blows the wind, and it is gone" is usually omitted.

Praise the Lord!
Marjorie Jillson, b. 1931
Source: *Five Hymns,* 1973
This hymn, based on Psalm 113, is one of five hymns written for tunes by the noted contemporary German composer, Heinz Werner Zimmermann (b. 1930). The theme of praise is highlighted by a jazz setting — which marks his style. The composer has indicated that the tempo should not be hurried.

Praise, the Lord, His glories show
Henry J. Lyte, 1793-1847
Source: *The Spirit of the Psalms,* 1834
The hymn, based on Psalm 150, originally consisted of two eight line stanzas, but is usually turned into four stanzas with added alleluas, so it can be sung to the popular Welsh tune, LLANFAIR. In *Hymns and Human Life,* Erik Routley wrote, "Lyte was an obscure country curate who has no claim to fame beyond his saintly character and a handful of hymns" — but his hymns are a lasting memorial.

Praise the Lord who reigns above
Charles Wesley, 1707-1788
Source: *A Collection of Psalms and Hymns,* 1743
Psalm 150 has inspired poets and composers in all generations with its references to the use of musical instruments to praise God. Charles' hymn was included in John's *Sunday Services,* which he sent in 1788 to be used by the American colonies. The meter is most unusual. Lines 1, 2 and 4 begin with an accent (trochaic), then shift midway to opposite (iambic). The effect is magical with its movement from sharpness of attack to gentleness of conclusion.

Praise the Lord! ye heavens, adore Him
Anon., 18th Century
Source: *The Foundling Hospital Collection,* 1796
This hymn has a curious background. In the late 18th century it was customary for wealthy Englishmen to ride in their carriages out to the "foundling hospitals" (we would call them orphanages) where they brought their gifts on Sunday afternoon. This hymn was pasted into some copies of a 1796 collection of 16 hymns called *Psalms and Hymns and Anthems of the Foundling Hospital.* It is based on Psalm 148 and contains two themes in two stanzas: God of Creation

in st. 1, and God of Salvation in st. 2.

Praise to God, immortal praise
Anna Laetitia Barbauld, 1743-1825
Source: *Hymns for Public Worship,* 1772
   It is easier to praise God in times of prosperity than in adversity, but the hymn by Mrs. Barbauld originally included stanzas for both themes. In its modern form adversity has been omitted, and only stanzas dealing with the theme of thanksgiving for all of the natural blessings of God are included. Thus it becomes a hymn for the harvest season.

Praise to the living God (The God of Abraham praise)
Based on the Yigdal of Daniel Ben Judah, 14th Century
Trans. Newton Mann, 1836-1926 and Max Landsberg, 1845-1928
   The *Yigdal* is a Jewish doxology codifying the 13 articles of the Jewish creed, giving it a Christian character. His hymn began "The God of Abraham praise." Around 1885 a Unitarian minister and a Jewish rabbi made a new metrical version, and it is their version which is usually included in hymnals, but sometimes beginning with Olivers' first line.

Praise to the Lord, the almighty, the King of creation
Joachim Neander, 1650-1680
Trans. Catherine Winkworth, 1827-1878
Source: *Glaub-und Liebes-übung,* 1680
   The hymn is based on Psalm 103:1-6 and Psalm 150:6, and is one of the most exuberant hymns of praise in the hymnal, due partly to its galloping dactyllic rhythm which allows fourteen syllables in each of the first two lines. It is highly probably that the author, who only lived 30 years, knew the tune as associated with an earlier chorale and wrote his outpouring of praise to Almighty God as Creator and Sovereign to provide new words.

Prayer is the soul's sincere desire
James Montgomery, 1771-1854
Source: *Treatise on Prayer,* 1819
   The hymn writer, Edward Bickersteth, asked the famous Moravian editor and hymn writer, James Montgomery, to write several hymns about prayer for his *Treatise on Prayer.* The author lists eleven aspects of prayer which are helpful in understanding the true meaning of prayer — a subject about which there is often much misunderstanding. The last stanza, with a reference to Jesus' affirmation, "I am the

Way, the Truth, and the Life," is a prayer to God to teach us how to pray.

Prepare the way to Zion
Frans Mikael Franzen, 1772-1847.
Trans. Composite, adapt. by Charles P. Price, b. 1920
Source: *Psalmbook,* 1819
 Franzen, who served with Archbishop Wallin in the preparation of the masterful Swedish *Psalmbook* of 1819, was born in Finland but lived most of his life in Sweden, where he served several churches before being appointed Bishop. The fine Advent text with echoes of Psalm 24:7-10 is graced with an ingratiating tune from another Swedish collection, *Then Swenska Psalmboken* of 1697.

Put forth, O Lord, Thy Spirit's power
Howard Chandler Robbins, 1876-1952
Source: *New Church Hymnal,* 1937
 The author, an Episcopalian who became Dean of the Cathedral of St. John the Divine in New York City and Professor of Pastoral Theology at General Theological Seminary, was a member of the editorial committee of the famous *Hymnal 1940.* This hymn is a fervent prayer for the Church, and is set in some hymnals to the tune CHELSEA SQUARE, which Robbins also wrote.

Rejoice, O land, in God thy might
Robert Seymour Bridges, 1844-1930
Source: *The Yattendon Hymnal,* 1897
 While many people change careers, it is not usual for a physician to give up his work to devote talents to literature, music, and hymnody; but this is what Bridges did, and we can be grateful to him for his contributions as editor of the notable *Yattendon Hymnal* (a book which was marked by the highest quality), his original hymns (this was based on Joel 2:21), and especially his fine translations. He was named poet laureate of England in 1913 in recognition of his outstanding contributions to literature.

Rejoice, O pilgrim throng!
(See: "Rejoice, ye pure in heart")

Rejoice, rejoice, believers
Laurentius Laurenti, 1660-1722
Trans. Sara Borthwick, 1823-1907
Source: *Evangelia Melodica,* 1700
 Laurenti, considered one of the finest of pietistic hymn writers,

wrote a set of texts and tunes for the entire church year. This hymn, based on Matthew 25:1-13 (the story of the wise and foolish virgins) originally was intended for a Sunday in Trinity, but it usually included in the Advent section. It is a call for us to be prepared to greet the Bridegroom (Jesus) whose coming is imminent.

Rejoice, the Lord is King
Charles Wesley, 1707-1788
Source: *Hymns for Our Lord's Resurrection,* 1746
   Although often sung for Ascension, the hymn was written for the theme of Easter, where Christ reigns victorious over sin and death. Therefore we "Rejoice" — the keynote of the hymn and of the refrain, based on Philippians 4:4 ("Rejoice in the Lord always; again I say, rejoice.") The famous composer, George F. Handel, wrote a tune GOPSAL (one of four he wrote for John Wesley) for this text, but it is usually sung to DARWALL, composed for Psalm 148.

Rejoice, ye pure in heart
Edward H. Plumptre, 1821-1891
Source: *Hymns Ancient and Modern,* Appendix, 1868
   Everyone enjoys a festival, and this hymn was written for a Diocesan Festival in Peterborough Cathedral in 1865. It originally contained eleven stanzas, necessary to get all of the choirs in. Based on Psalm 20:4, Psalm 147:1, and Philippians 4:4, it is call for youth, the elderly, men, maidens — everyone to rejoice.

Renew Thy church, her ministries restore
Kenneth Cober, b. 1902
Source: *American Baptist Convention,* May 1960
   The author, son of missionary parents, grew up in Puerto Rico but has spent a large part of his ministry in Christian Education assignments in the American Baptist Church. In 1960, as part of the Baptist Jubilee Advance, it was first used as a theme hymn for church renewal in the denomination. It is a call for the church to restore its ministries to a renewed commitment to the Gospel.

Ride on, ride on in majesty
Henry H. Milman, 1791-1868
Source: *Hymns Written and Adapted to the Weekly Service of the Church Year,* 1827
   "The Sixth Sunday in Lent" (the hymn's heading) is Palm Sunday, and the author, who became Dean of St. Paul's in London, wrote the hymn while he was Professor of Poetry at Oxford. The theme of the entire hymn is "Majesty", and Milman presents the Passion

of Christ with royalty and sees the cross in terms of victory rather than defeat. It is an effective presentation of the dual themes of Palm Sunday: meekness and majesty, sacrifice and conquest, suffering and glory.

Rise up, O men of God
William P. Merrill, 1867-1954
Source: *Continent,* 1911

This is a hymn written specifically for men and inspired by the need of a brotherhood hymn for the Presbyterian Brotherhood Movement. The author was a famous Presbyterian pastor in Chicago, who later became one of three hymn writers to serve Brick Presbyterian Church in New York City — the others being Henry Van Dyke and Maltbie D. Babcock.

Rock of ages, cleft for me
Augustus M. Toplady, 1740-1778
Source: *Gospel Magazine,* 1775

This is a hymn about sin and salvation, about our helpless need, and about the all-sufficiency of Christ's atonement. The metaphor of the Rock of Ages is found variously in Isaiah 26:4, Exodus 33:22, I Corinthians 10:4. Strongly Calvinist, Toplady carried on a running public feud for years with John Wesley, even calling him ''a low and puny tadpole in the sea of divinity.'' Fortunately his hymn does not carry any of this mean spirit.

Savior, again to Thy dear name we raise
John Ellerton, 1826-1893
Source: Appendix to *Hymns Ancient and Modern,* 1868

England in the 19th century was famous for its choral societies, and this hymn was written for an 1866 choral festival. As a closing hymn it is a prayer for the peace of God — on our way home, through the night, and at the end of our earthly life.

Savior, like a shepherd lead us
Anon. (Attr. to Dorothy A. Thrupp, 1779-1847)
Source: *Hymns for the Young,* 1836

In the 19th century hymnal editors often failed to identify authors. Dorothy Thrupp in the first edition of this collection (1836) left all hymns unsigned, and since women often were loathe to press their cause it is possible that the text is hers. The words are based on the idea of Jesus as Shepherd plus a few ideas from Psalm 23. It was intended for children rather than adults.

Savior of the nations, come
St. Ambrose, 340-397
Trans. (Paraphrase) Martin Luther, 1483-1546
Trans. to English, William M. Reynolds, 1812-1876
Source: 8th and 9th Century manuscripts
    The bishop of Milan is known as the father of Latin hymnody. His hymn rings the keynote for Advent, with the seven stanzas providing opportunity to proclaim God's purpose in sending the Messiah and our response to this Good News. Martin Luther's German translation, "Num komm, der heiden Heiland," was put into English by William M. Reynolds, son of a captain in the Revolutionary War.

See the conqueror mounts in triumph
Christopher Wordsworth, 1807-1885
Source: *The Holy Year,* 1862
    In the new hymnal edited by Erik Routley, *Rejoice in the Lord,* eight scriptural references are given for this hymn of the Ascension of Christ: Psalm 24:7, Psalm 98:2, Luke 24:50-51, Genesis 5:24, Hebrews 5:4, Joshua 5:1, II Kings 2:9-11; Hebrews 1:5-8. This indicates the rich Biblical imagery which the nephew of the poet William Wordsworth uses to give the sense of splendor and majesty of Christ's ascending to heaven after the Resurrection.

Shepherd of Souls
(See: "Be known to us in breaking bread")
Anon.
Source: *A Collection of Hymns,* 1832
    This two stanza hymn, first published in a United Brethren hymnal in 1832 is sometimes combined with Montgomery's two stanza hymn, "Be known to us in breaking bread." Since both hymns deal with the themes of spiritual refreshment (manna and water in the desert; bread and cup at the table) they can be combined, although only the Montgomery text deals with the Lord's Supper.

Silent night, holy night
Joseph Mohr, 1792-1848. Trans. John F. Young, 1820-1885
Source: *Leipziger Gesangbuch,* 1838
    The church organ at Oberndorf, Austria, had broken down on Christmas Eve, so Pastor Mohr jotted down the poem beginning "Stille Nacht, heilige Nacht!" in six stanzas and asked organist Gruber if he could write a melody for it. So it was sung Christmas Eve with a choir of village girls singing the melody, Mohr playing guitar and singing tenor, and Gruber singing bass. From such a simple

beginning came our most beloved Christmas hymn.

Sing, my tongue, the glorious battle
St. Thomas Aquinas, c. 1225-1274
Trans. John M. Neale, 1818-1866
Source: *Hymns for all the Festivals of the Christian Year.* n. d.

For the liturgy of Corpus Christi (The Body of Christ) Pope Urban IV asked Aquinas to write this hymn, originally in ten stanzas and often divided into two separate hymns. Thus divided it was sung at Matins (after midnight) and Lauds (sunrise) each day from Passion Sunday until Maundy Thursday. The original Latin is quite complicated and there are at least six major translations in use during Holy Week.

Sing of Mary, pure and lowly
Roland Ford Palmer, b. 1891
Source: Canadian *Book of Common Prayer,* 1938

Based on an anonymous poem published in an Ilkeston, Derbyshire pamphlet c. 1914, and inspired by the need for a devotional hymn for the Feast of the Annunciation, Roland F. Palmer (born in London, but a Canadian resident since 1905) wrote this hymn to emphasize the spiritual rather more than the physical aspects of the Annunciation. Its theme is Mary and Jesus — her love for Him and His love for her. *The Hymnal 1940* (Episcopal) was the first to include it as a congregational hymn.

Sing praise to God who reigns above
Johann J. Schuetz, 1640-1690
Trans. Frances E. Cox, 1812-1897
Source: *Christliches Gedenchbüchlein,* 1675

The hymn by the successful Frankfurt lawyer was based on Deuteronomy 32:3 ("because I will publish the name of the Lord: ascribe ye greatness unto our God"). The text speaks eloquently of God's creation, power, love, salvation, mercy and providence with a closing call to remind all Christians that the glory belongs to God — a theme of which Jesus kept reminding his listeners. The tune is based on motives found in other tunes of the time, and with its uneven number of phrases (5) and its long held gathering note for each phrase compels and impels the singer through one of the most enjoyable tunes in the hymnals.

Sing to the Lord of harvest
John Samuel Bewley Monsell, 1811-1875
Source: *Hymns of Love and Praise,* 1866

In a day when hymn singing was purposely restrained and proper, Monsell urged that hymns be "more fervent and joyous. We are too distant and reserved in our praises; we sing, not as we should sing to Him who is Chief among ten thousand, the Altogether Lovely." Certainly harvest time should be a time of thanks-singing and thanksgiving. The author was accidently killed by falling stonework when his church of St. Nicholas was being rebuilt.

Sing with all the sons (saints) of glory
William J. Irons, 1812-1883
Source: *Psalms and Hymns for the Church,* 1873
The Anglican rector and prebendary of St. Paul's Cathedral, London, printed his hymn under the text "Now is Christ risen from the dead" (I Corinthians 15:20). It is an exuberant and exhilarating hymn about the meaning of the resurrection, with echoes of the book of Revelation. Written in the popular meter of 87.87.D. it is singable to a number of favorite hymn tunes so that it can easily be sung by the once-a-year Easter visitors!

Soldiers of Christ, arise
Charles Wesley, 1707-1788
Source: *The Character of a Methodist,* 1742
The hymn is based on Ephesians 6:10-18 where the apostle describes the Christian life as a spiritual conflict with evil and exhorts us to "Put on the whole armor of God." The Greek word "panoply" means "whole armor." God provides the armor; we have to take it all and put it on. All life is a battle with evil, and the Church on earth is always the Church militant.

Sometimes a light surprises
William Cowper, 1731-1800
Source: *Olney Hymns,* 1779
Cowper, whose struggles with dark moments of the soul are well documented, entitled this cheerful hymn "Joy and peace in believing." It is based on Matthew 6:34 ("Take therefore no thought for the morrow") and Habakkuk 3:17-18 (though all goes wrong, yet I will rejoice in the Lord). Filled with Biblical language (there are also references to Malachi 4:2, II Samuel 23:4, and Matthew 6), all of its metaphors are drawn from the world of nature. This is a good hymn to refer to whenever you find yourself worrying and becoming anxious.

Son of God, eternal Savior
Somerset Corry Lowry, 1855-1932

Source: *Christian Social Union Hymn Book,* 1895

There are social implications in the gospel which are often over-looked or ignored by those who feel that a personal relationship to Christ is all that is necessary. Lowry's hymn reminds us that we have a common bond with the whole human race through Christ, that a life of service is required of our stewardship, and that we must pray for peace to end our strife and shame our selfish greed. Our prayer is always "Thy will be done."

Songs of thankfulness and praise
Christopher Wordsworth, 1807-1885
Source: *The Holy Year,* 1862

"Epiphany" means "manifestation" of Christ to the world, and the author used the word "manifest" twelve times to describe Christ's birth, baptism, appearance at the wedding feast in Cana, healing the sick, and his powers over evil. Thus the hymn becomes not only praise to God, but a time for learning more about Epiphany and about Christ himself.

Soul, adorn yourself with gladness.
(See: Deck thyself, my soul, with gladness)

Spirit divine, accept our prayers
Andrew Reed, 1787-1862
Source: *Evangelical Magazine,* June 1829

In 1829 the Board of Congregational Ministers in London urged the appointment of a special day (Good Friday) of humiliation and prayer to promote a revival of religion in British churches. The hymn was written for that occasion. The text was radically revised by Samuel Longfellow for American use in *Hymns of the Spirit* (1864). Although stanza one suggests the theme of dedicating a new church, the rest of the hymn is a prayer for renewal by the Holy Spirit, to come as light, fire, and a dove to awaken the Church to new life.

Spirit of God, descend upon my heart
George Croly, 1780-1860
Source: *Lyra Britannica,* 1867

Some hymn writers such as Watts and Wesley are remembered for many great hymns, but most writers are lucky if only one hymn survives. This by Croly, based on Galatians 5:25 ("If we live in the Spirit, let us also walk in the Spirit"), is a very intense and personal prayer for God's Spirit to take over our life, purify it, and fill it with the pure love of angels. The last line is particularly appealing: "My heart an altar, and thy love the flame."

Stand up and bless the Lord
James Montgomery, 1771-1854
Source: *Christian Psalmist,* 1825
The text is based on Nehemiah 9:5 ("Stand up and bless the Lord your God forever and ever") and was written by the famous Moravian newspaper editor and hymn writer for a Wesleyan Sunday school anniversary. Like "Spirit of God, descend upon my heart" and Wesley's "O Thou who camest from above," it includes the picture of an altar and the living flame from God touching our lives.

Stand up, stand up for Jesus
George Duffield, Jr., 1818-1888
Source: *The Psalmist,* 1858
A young minister, Dudley Tyng of Philadelphia, preaching at a YMCA prayer meeting exhorted the 5,000 men present to "Stand up for Jesus." The following Wednesday he caught his sleeve in a horse-pulled corn sheller, his arm was torn away, and he died within hours. The next Sunday the famous Presbyterian preacher, Duffield, preaching from Ephesians 6:14 ("Stand therefore, having your loins girt about with truth") concluded with this hymn based on Tyng's exhortation, and written especially for the day.

Strengthen for service, Lord
Liturgy of Malabar, 5th Century
Trans. Percy Dearmer, 1867-1936
Source: *The English Hymnal,* 1906
The story of this hymn begins with a 5th century prayer in the ancient Church of St. Thomas in Malabar, South India, said while people were receiving communion. Neale, the noted English hymn scholar-translator, made a version in prose, which Charles Humphreys put into verse. Finally Dearmer, the editor of *The English Hymnal* (1906), made a few alterations and included it in that hymnal. Partaking of the communion meal is not an escape from the world: the supper is a preparation for it and sanctifying the whole of life.

Strong Son of God, immortal Love
Alfred Tennyson, 1809-1892
Source: Prologue to *In Memoriam,* 1849
This text was never meant by Tennyson to be sung. Rather, it was an invocation, a prologue, and overview of a series of elegiac poems which Tennyson wrote after the tragic death of his friend and prospective brother-in-law, Arthur Henry Hallam. At the time of death we must go on faith and faith alone, for our mortal minds cannot comprehend the purpose or the ways of God.

Sun of my soul, Thou Savior dear
John Keble, 1792-1866
Source: *Christian Year,* 1827

Originally an evening hymn beginning, "'Tis gone, that bright and orbed blaze," it was inspired by Luke 24:29 ("Abide with us: for it is toward evening, and the day is far spent"). While it is a prayer for rest at night, it is also a prayer for Christ's presence both in life and death. It is also a prayer for others — for wandering sinners, the sick, the poor, the mourning. And like most evening hymns it closes with a prayer that we shall wake after death to a new life in heaven.

Take my life, and let it be consecrated
Frances R. Havergal, 1836-1879
Source: *Songs of Grace and Glory,* 1874

Miss Havergal during a visit with friends prayed that God would use her witness to win all ten members of the family to Christ. "Before I left the house everyone had got a blessing," she wrote. On the last night of her visit twelve couplets came to her mind dealing with true consecration, which involves mind, body, words, deeds, intellect, will, money, possession, and the whole self. The final couplet integrates and sums up these with *"Ever, only, ALL for Thee!"*

Take up thy cross", the Savior said
Charles W. Everest, 1814-1877
Source: *Visions of Death and Other Poems,* 1833

The author, a minister in the Episcopal Church, wrote his hymn as a youth of nineteen. Jesus spoke to his disciples in Mark 8:34 about the necessity for taking up the cross and following, and Everest's hymn describes the fully committed Christian life as denying self, renouncing the world, bearing the shame of the cross, facing all dangers, and following Christ to the uttermost. True discipleship is costly!

Tell out, my soul, the greatness of the Lord
Timothy Dudley-Smith, b. 1926
Source: *Anglican Hymn Book* 1965

The opening line is based on the New English Bible version of the Magnificat, Mary's song when she learned from the angel that she was to be the mother of Jesus. The whole song is found in Luke 1:46-55. Bishop Dudley-Smith of the Anglican Church is one of the leading contemporary hymn writers, having contributed many hymns to *Youth Praise* (1966) and *Psalm Praise* (1974)

Thanks to God, whose Word was spoken
R. T. Brooks, b. 1918
Source: *The Methodist Hymnal*, 1966

Since 1950 "Peter" Brooks was with the British Broadcasting Corporation in radio, television, and religious broadcasting. His hymn was written in 1954 for the Triple Jubilee of the British and Foreign Bible Society, and the theme of the hymn is "thanks" or "praise" for the Word of God — in the Old Testament stories of creation and founding Israel, in the birth of the incarnate Word in Jesus, in the revelations of the Scriptures, in translations in many different tongues, and in the Spirit's voice within us. God's Word is always an open word. God is still speaking!

That Easter Day with joy was bright
Anon. Latin, 4th or 5th Century
Trans. John M. Neale, 1818-1866
Source: "Aurora lucis rutilat"

The hymn has sometimes been ascribed to St. Ambrose, and is one of the earlier to be adopted for a special season. Although written in classical, austere Long Meter (four lines of poetry, each with eight syllables), it is usually sung to a jubilant triple time tune, PUER NOBIS, from the 15th century. The stanzas usually included in a hymnal are basically praise, while four other stanzas usually omitted deal with the Easter narrative in more detail.

The glory of these forty days
Gregory the Great, c. 540-604
Trans. Maurice F. Bell, 1862-1947
Source: Latin, 6th century

The Latin hymn *Clarum decus jejunii* may have been written by Gregory the Great. A hymn for the opening of the Lenten season, it is a reminder of the necessity for fasting and prayer as exemplified by Moses, Elijah, Daniel and John the Baptist.

The Head that once was crowned with thorns
Thomas Kelly, 1769-1854
Source: *Hymns on Various Passages of Scriptures,* 1820

Under the title "Perfect through sufferings" (Hebrews 2:10), the hymn is the story of two crownings of Jesus — the first by the Roman soldiers in mock tribute and the later vision of John where Christ wears many crowns (Revelation 19:12). While many Evangelical hymns of his time have been radically altered, Kelly's hymn is so skillfully written that it has always escaped the hymnal editor's scalpel.

The heavens declare Thy glory, Lord
Isaac Watts, 1674-1748
Source: *Psalms of David, Imitated in the Language of the New Testament,* 1719
This paraphrase of Psalm 19 was headed "The Books of Nature and of Scripture Compared; or, The Glory and Success of the Gospel." Though Watts saw that the purpose of the psalmist was to "show the Excellence of the Book of Scripture above the Book of Nature," he also felt that Romans 10:18 with its reference to the gospel going into all the world made it mandatory that his psalm paraphrase end with the message of Christ, and the Gospel revealed as greater than God's revelation in nature.

The King of Love my Shepherd is
Henry W. Baker, 1821-1877
Source: Appendix to *Hymns Ancient and Modern,* 1868
Baker's hymn is not just another metrical version or paraphrase of Psalm 23, but rather treats it freely and gives it a distinctively Christian framework. Christ, the Good Shepherd, is the center of the setting, and the Cross, (a symbol of Christ's laying down his life for the sheep) is followed by a sacramental emphasis on the Lord's table and the eucharistic chalice. You might enjoy comparing this setting with "The Lord's my Shepherd," "In heavenly love abiding," and "Savior, like a shepherd lead us."

The King shall come when morning dawns
Anon. Greek Hymn. Trans. John Brownlie, 1857-1925
Source: *Hymns from the East,* 1907
No Greek source for this hymn has ever been found, and it is possible that it was an original hymn by Brownlie, a Scotsman whose translations were admired by John Julian, the author of *Dictionary of Hymnology.* However, the thoughts of the hymn certainly reflect the early Greek emphasis on light and salvation. The last stanza ends with a translation of the famous second-coming phrase, "Maranatha" — "Even so, Lord Jesus, quickly come!".

The living God my shepherd is
J. Driscoll, SJ, d. 1940
Brother James' Air is one of those haunting melodies that is a perennial favorite of choirs. In recent years it has begun to appear in books as a hymn tune, usually with the Psalm 23 paraphrase of the *Scottish Psalter* of 1650. Driscoll's paraphrase with its inner rhyme in line five (day-way, bide-guide, etc.) effectively avoids the repetition of text which earlier versions needed to fit the tune.

The Lord will come and not be slow
John Milton, 1608-1674
Source: *Nine of the Psalms Done into Metre,* 1648

At one time in England it was the fashion to paraphrase the psalms as close to the word order of the Hebrew as possible. The famous English poet, Milton, to reassure the readers that his versions were authentic, put Hebrew words in the margin and printed every English word not found in the original text in italics. He set Psalms 80 to 88 and, from these, various stanzas have been selected and put into modern hymn form for singing.

The Lord's my Shepherd, I'll not want
Psalm 23
Source: *Scottish Psalter,* 1650

The *Scottish Psalter* of 1650 has been called the "Prince of Versions" because it contains the cream of all the best psalters up to that time. This psalm version includes parts from at least seven different psalters, distilled into the most famous paraphrase of the most popular psalm.

The royal banners forward go
Venantius Fortunatus, c. 530-609
Trans. John Mason Neale, 1818-1866
Source: *Medieval Hymns,* 1851

For the consecreation of a new nunnery in Poitiers, Queen Rhadegunda procured relics of the "true cross" from Emperor Justin II. They travelled from Tours in a procession of barges lit with torches, with the Queen and Bishop Fortunatus heading it for the last three miles. The arrival of this procession on November 19, 569, was the first time this hymn was sung. Upon the cross as throne Christ rules and wins our allegiance.

The Son of God goes forth to war
Reginald Heber, 1783-1826
Source: *Hymns Written and Adapted to the Weekly Service of the Church Year,* 1827

St. Stephen's Day is the day following Christmas, and commemorates the first Christian martyr — stoned to death while Saul (later Paul) stood by and watched the coats of the murderers. While stanza two refers directly to this event, the rest of the hymn commemorates the twelve disciples who also faced peril, toil, and pain to follow the blood-red banner of Christ. Are we willing to follow Christ with their depth of commitment?

The Church of Christ in every age
Fred Pratt Green, b. 1903
Source: *Hymns and Songs,* 1969
The author is well known for his willingness and enthusiasm in writing hymns "on demand" for special occasions. In 1967 he received a request from the Methodist hymnal committee of Great Britain for "a hymn which tackled the relationship of Sabbath and Sunday." His willingness also to make alterations is reflected in his comment about *Lutheran Book of Worship* when it included this hymn, "The changes asked for by *your* committee have improved it." This is a powerful hymn about the mission of the Church.

The Church's one foundation
Samuel J. Stone, 1839-1900
Source: *Lyra Fidelium,* 1866
A mid-19th century controversy over a new way of studying and interpreting scripture advocated by Bishop Colenso of Natal was the source of this hymn, a defense of the traditional way of interpretation. The stanza which includes the lines, "By schisms rent asunder, By heresies distrest", is now usually omitted. Christ is the foundation (I Corinthians 3:11), its members are his "new creation" (II Corinthians 5:17), and they are his "holy bride" for whom he gave his life (Ephesians 5:25). It is the most familiar statement about the church in hymn literature.

The day of resurrection
John of Damascus, c. 657-c.749. Trans. John M. Neale, 1818-1866
Source: *Hymns of the Eastern Church,* 1862
This is a translation of Ode I in the Golden Canon of Easter — a Greek hymn from before the 8th century. It is sung in Greek churches at midnight before Easter as the congregation lights candles to dispel darkness and the silence is shatterd by sounds of drums and trumpets. The hymn moves from the Exodus (crossing the Red Sea appears in all Greek Easter hymns) to the New Testament story of Easter morning, ending with a call to all to be joyful and to rejoice.

The day Thou gavest, Lord, is ended
John Ellerton, 1826-1893
Source: *A Liturgy for Missionary Meetings,* 1870
This is both an evening and missionary hymn, but its main theme is the growing world wide fellowship of the Church, which offers unbroken, unceasing praise and prayer. Thus it is most appropriate for use on World Wide Communion Sunday. Queen Victoria chose it for her Diamond Jubilee in 1897, but the final stanza reminds us

that while "earth's proud empires pass away," God's Kingdom is forever.

The duteous day now closeth
Paul Gerhardt, 1607-1676
Trans. Robert Seymour Bridges, 1844-1930
(Now all the woods are sleeping)
Trans. Catherine Winkworth, 1827-1878
Source: *Praxis Pietatis Melica,* 1648

Gerhardt, second only to Luther as a German hymn writer, combined elements of the older, objective type of hymnody with a newer, more subjective type which was popular with the Pietists. This evening hymn is perhaps the most beautiful prayer at eventide in all hymnody, enhanced by the famous Heinrich Isaac tune (originally set to "Innsbruck, I leave thee sadly") which Johann S. Bach adapted as a hymn tune.

The first Nowell the angel did say
Traditional English Carol, 17th Century
Source: *Some Ancient Christmas Carols,* 1823

The word "Nowell" (Noel-Nadal-Natal-Natale) derives from the Latin "Natalis,"meaning birthday or birth. Chaucer in the 14th century "Canterbury Tales" in "The Franklin's Tale" wrote, "And 'Nowel' cryeth every lusty man." The narrative carol sometimes has the details of the Christmas story slightly confused, but the most unusual tune (which may have been a descant to some other carol) is so much fun that no one objects.

The spacious firmament on high
Joseph Addison, 1672-1719
Source: *Spectator,* August 23, 1712

The author's literary fame rests on his contributions to four newspapers, including the *Spectator* which he founded in 1711 and in which all of his hymns appeared. The hymn is taken from the end of a discourse on the proper means of strengthening and confirming faith. He wrote, "The Supreme Being has made the best arguments for his own existence in the formation of the heavens and the earth. . . ." Then followed his paraphrase of Psalm 19:1-6, which is often sung to Franz Josef Haydn's melody from "The Creation."

The strife is o'er, the battle done
Anon. Latin, 17th Century. Trans. Francis Pott, 1832-1909
Source: *Symphonia Sirena Selectarum,* 1695

Pott, a member of the original committee for the monumental

Hymns Ancient and Modern (1861), made his translation from a Latin hymn with three lines of text in eight syllables, followed by Allelua. The simple, straightforward Easter text is suitably set to a tune based on a "Gloria Patri" from Palestrina's *Magnificat Tertii Toni* (1591). It is one of the simplest tunes in the hymnal, but one of the most effective.

There is a balm in Gilead
Negro Spiritual

It is probable that this spiritual grew out of slaves' experience of hymns by Charles Wesley and John Newton, for both used the phrase "sin-sick soul." In Jeremiah 8:22 the question is asked, "Is there no balm in Gilead?" and the expected answer is "No." But the spiritual turns the negative into affirmation, and hopelessness into hope. The balm of Gilead may have been from a local tree or bought from Eastern Caravans passing through, but the balm of the spiritual is Christ.

There is a green hill far away
Cecil Frances Alexander, 1818-1895
Source: *Hymns for Little Children,* 1848

Mrs. Alexander's hymns were written to make the articles of the Apostles' Creed meaningful for the children in Sunday school. This text was designed to explain "Suffered under Pontius Pilate; was crucified, dead and buried." The last stanza is the heart of the hymn as it presents the purpose, the necessity and the challenge of the cross.

There's a wideness in God's mercy
Frederick W. Faber, 1814-1863
Source: *Oratory Hymns,* 1854

Of Huguenot ancestry and strict training in Calvinism, Faber moved from priesthood in the Anglican Church to the Roman Catholic Church in 1846. He wrote 150 hymns, corresponding to the number of psalms. He tried to emulate William Cowper, John Newton, and the Wesleys, and this hymn in part matches their simplicity and evangelical fervor. Originally in 13 stanzas, the hymn was called "Come to Jesus" and began "Souls of men, why will ye scatter like a crowd of frightened sheep?"

Thine arm, O Lord, in days of old
Edward H. Plumptre, 1821-1891
Source: *Lazarus and Other Poems,* 1865

The author won fame as a scholar, theologian and preacher, and held many prestigious postions including Dean of Wells Cathedral.

He was a member of the Old Testament Company for the revision of the Authorized Version of the Bible. This hymn was written in 1864 for use in the Chapel of King's College Hospital and is one of the finest about health and healing.

Thine be (is) the glory
Edmond L. Budry, 1854-1932
Trans. R. Birch Hoyle, 1875-1939
Source: *Chants Evangeliques,* 1885
The French hymn was written to be sung to the chorus "See, the conquering hero comes" from *Judas Maccabaeus,* an oratorio composed by George F. Handel at the suggestion of the Prince of Wales. It was translated into English for the polyglot *Cantate Domino* (1924) for use by the World Student Christian Federation. All hymns were in at least English, French and German (plus other languages for certain hymns) so that they could be used in international meetings with each person singing in his or her native tongue.

This is my Father's world
Maltbie D. Babcock, 1858-1901
Source: *Thoughts for Every-Day Living,* 1901
The author, a handsome and popular Presbyterian minister, often used to leave his home for an early morning walk up a hill overlooking Lake Ontario saying, "I am going out to see my Father's world." The hymn text is one of the finest nature hymns and is enhanced by Franklin Sheppard's arrangement of an English folk tune. In some hymnals the last stanza has been replaced by a stanza written much later by the author's daughter, Mary Babcock Crawford.

This joyful Eastertide
George Ratcliffe Woodward, 1848-1934
Source: *Carols for Easter and Ascension,* 1894
The author, a gifted translator of Latin, Greek and German hymns, edited a number of collections of carols including folk tunes from many world sources. The Dutch tune VRUECHTEN was a popular 17th century Dutch song, and for it Woodward provided his original words which have become increasingly popular. Fred Pratt Green, retired British Methodist minister, has also provided a different text for the tune, but beginning with the same first line.

Thou art the Way: to Thee alone
George W. Doane, 1799-1859
Source: *Songs by the Way,* 1824
This is the first American hymn to find wide acceptance in England.

Bishop Doane of New Jersey was a distinguished scholar, church leader, and man of letters. His inspiration was the words of Jesus, "I am the way, the truth, and the life" (John 14:6), and it is an example of an "itemized hymn". Each of the three words is developed in single stanzas, with the final stanza summing up in the form of a prayer.

Thou hidden Love of God, whose height
Gerhardt Tersteegen, 1697-1769
Trans. John Wesley, 1703-1791
Source: *Geistliches Blumengärtlein inniger Seelen,* 1729

Wesley on his early trip to America on shipboard with Moravians was deeply impressed with their piety and especially their calmness and trust in God as they sang hymns during a violent storm. In Savannah he began to translate some of their hymns, and Tersteegen's hymn titled "The Longing of the Soul quietly to maintain the secret drawings of the Love of God" expressed the longing Wesley had in his soul — his conversion experience came after returning to England. The last line of stanza one, "My heart is pained, nor can it be At rest till it finds rest in Thee" is not in the original German, but is drawn from the well-known passage in Augustine's *Confessions.*

Thou Judge, by whom each empire fell
Percy Dearmer, 1867-1936
Source: *Songs of Praise,* 1925

With Ralph Vaughan Williams, Percy Dearmer edited the monumental *English Hymnal* (1906) and later collaborated again to produce *Songs of Praise* (1925). While he is most famous for his hymnal editing, he also wrote several hymns. This was written "in an attempt to express what is felt to be the truth about the idea of judgment, and also because there were not enough hymns to carry the great tunes in this meter", thus recognizing and expressing the truth that the tune is equally important to a hymn.

Thou whose almighty Word
John Marriott, 1780-1825
Source: *Evangelical Magazine,* June 1825

Missionary movements have often been the inspiration for hymns, and this was titled "Missionary Hymn" but printed anonymously in the *Evangelical Magazine* of June 1825. Its scriptural basis is Genesis 1:1-4, but the framework is Trinitarian. God created light, Christ was the Light of the world, and the Holy Spirit continues to shed light, and the hymn prays that this light may be shed abroad everywhere.

Through all the changing scenes of life
Nahum Tate, 1652-1715 and Nicolaus Brady, 1659-1726
Source: *New Version of the Psalms of David,* 1696
Two Irishmen edited the *New Version* of the psalms to replace the *Old Version* of Sternhold and Hopkins (1562). Both men were chaplains to William III. Most of their paraphrases have disappeared from modern hymnals, but this version of Psalm 34 (originally in 22 stanzas) has a directness and beauty which is enhanced by the fine tune IRISH which first appeared in a collection of tunes for John Wesley, edited by a bassoon player named John Lampe in Handel's orchestra.

Through the night of doubt and sorrow
Bernhardt Severin Ingemann, 1789-1862
Trans. Sabine Baring-Gould 1834-1924
Source: *Nyt Tillaeg til Evangelisk-chrestlig Psalmebog,* 1859
The Danish author of this hymn was both a scholar and a writer of popular historical novels modeled after those by Sir Walter Scott. He also edited the official Danish hymnal of 1859, where the hymn first appeared. The imagery is that of the Israelite's journey to the promised land, given a Christian interpretation, and applied to the pilgrim Church on earth. The use of the word "one" is paramount: one goal, one faith, one hope, one song, one conflict, one march, and one song of gladness at the end of the journey.

Thy Kingdom come, O Lord
Frederick L. Hosmer, 1840-1929
Source: *Hymn and Tune Book,* 1904
The Unitarian author of this hymn wrote two texts beginning with the same opening three words — based on the second petition of the Lord's Prayer. Both hymns emphasize world peace. Hosmer, who served both Congregational and Unitarian churches in five states, was one of the most gifted Unitarian hymn writers in America, and was invited to present lectures on hymnology at the Harvard Divinity School in 1908.

Thy strong word did cleave the darkness
Martin H. Franzmann, 1907-1976
Source: *Worship Supplement to The Lutheran Hymnal,* 1969
Franzmann wrote this text in 1954 for Concordia Seminary, St. Louis, and based it on the seminary motto "Anothen to Phos" (From the Light). It is a powerful, positive text on the strength of God's

Word — in creation, in sending salvation, in redemption on the cross, and in sanctification. Notice stanza five in which all of our body vocal parts are called upon to sing "Alleluas without end!"

'Tis midnight, and on Olive's brow
William B. Tappan, 1794-1849
Source: *Poems*, 1822

Based on Mark 14:32-42, the hymn is a description of the agonies of Christ praying in the garden of Gethsemane, alone with his griefs while the disciples slept. The author was a clock maker first in Boston, and then in Philadelphia where he became a Congregational minister and evangelist. Of ten volumes of verse, this is his only hymn to survive.

To God be the glory! great things He hath done!
Fanny Crosby, 1820-1915
Source: *Brightest and Best*, 1875

Fanny Crosby probably is the most popular and widely sung hymn author in America. The blind author's gospel song was not included in the famous *Gospel Hymns* 1-6 published by Ira D. Sankey and did not become popular in America until it was included in the song book for the Billy Graham Greater London Crusade in 1954.

To mock your reign, O dearest Lord
Fred Pratt Green, b. 1903
Source: *Sixteen Hymns of Today*, 1973

This is a hymn for Holy Week based on Mark 15:17-20. The first half of each stanza depicts the mock symbols (crown of thorns, purple cloak, sceptered reed) of Christ's passion. But the soldiers could not know as we do now that these symbols would be glorified and hallowed by Christ through his suffering and resurrection.

To Thee before the close of day
Latin, 7th Century. Trans. John David Chambers, 1805-1893,
    and John Mason Neale, 1818-1866
Source: *Psalter, or Seven Ordinary Hours of Sarum*, 1852

This hymn has been used throughout the Western Church since very ancient times, always in the last service of the day, Compline. It is a smple prayer for God's guidance and protection through the night.

Turn back, O man, forswear thy foolish ways
Clifford Bax, 1886-1962
Source: *Motherland Song Book*, 1919

The famous English composer Gustav Holst requested Bax to write a poem to fit the tune GENEVA 124 for a special arrangement for chorus and orchestra. The text is a clarion call for mankind to turn from its evil ways and to bring peace on the earth. Its goal is the time when "God's whole will be done" (on earth as it is in heaven.)

'Twas on that dark and doleful night (See: "It happened on that fateful night")

Unto us a boy is born
Anon. Latin Hymn. Trans. Percy Dearmer, 1867-1936
Source: *Trier Manuscript,* 15th Century
During the Middle Ages the final syllable of Alleluia was often treated with a florid melody consisting of many extra notes. In order to make these easier to remember, extra words were added, a method called troping. "Puer Nobis Nascitur" was a popular Christmas trope, telling the story of Jesus' birth.

Unto the hills around do I lift up my longing eyes
John Douglas Sutherland Campbell, 1845-1914
Source: *The Book of Psalms,* 1877
Using the meter of the familiar hymn, "Lead, kindly Light," the ninth Duke of Argyll, Governor-General of Canada, and son-in-law of Queen of Victoria wrote a collection of psalm paraphrases, of which this is his version of Psalm 121.

Wake, awake, for night is flying
Philipp Nicolai, 1556-1608
Trans. Catherine Winkworth, 1827-1878
Source: *Freuden-Spiegel des ewigen Lebens,* 1599
Sometimes called the "King of Chorales," the hymn is titled "Of the Voice at Midnight, and the wise Virgins who meet their Heavenly Bridegroom" based on Matthew 25:1-13 with other references to Revelation 19:6, Revelation 21:21, I Corinthians 2:9, Ezekiel 3:17, and Isaiah 52:8. Nicolai, who also composed the famous melody, wrote his hymns as meditations on death and eternal life in the midst of the pestilence in Westphalia in which over 1,300 people died in six months.

Watchman, tell us of the night
John Bowring, 1792-1872
Source: *Hymns,* 1825
The author uses the imagery of a traveller (he himself travelled extensively in business and was Governor of Hong Kong) to recreate

in dialogue form the longings expressed in Isaiah 21:11-12. The question and answer format makes it useful for antiphonal singing.

We all believe in one true God
Tobias Clausnitzer, 1619-1684
Trans. Catherine Winkworth, 1827-1878
Source: Culmbach-Bayreuth *Gesangbuch,* 1668

Luther's German paraphrase of the Apostles' Creed was long and involved, so this shorter and simpler form was written to replace it by the Lutheran Chaplain to the Swedish Army during the Thirty Years; War. The words paraphrase the three main articles of the Creed about God, Christ, and the Holy Spirit.

We come unto our fathers' God
Thomas Hornblower Gill, 1819-1906
Source: *Golden Chain of Praise Hymns,*1869

The author wrote that he was inspired to write this hymn by what he called "my lively delight in my Protestant forefathers" — hence the reference to "our fathers' God" in the first line. The God of our ancestors is still our God, our rock, our salvation, our dwelling place, our guide, our strength, and our joy. It is our responsibility to hand on to the next generation our faith and our joy so that the song will never end.

We gather together to ask the Lord's blessing
Netherlands Folk Hymn. Trans. Theodore Baker, 1851-1934
Source: *Nederlandtsch Gedenckclanck,* 1626

The original Dutch text was a patriotic song written at the end of the 16th century to celebrate the release of the Netherlands from Spanish rule. Its theme is the providence of God and the prayer "O Lord, make us free!" Edward Kremser, director of a male choral society in Vienna, first arranged the old folksong for men's voices.

We give Thee but Thine own
William W. How, 1823-1897
Source: *Psalms and Hymns,* 1864

Bishop How, an Anglican, presents effectively the meaning of stewardship. All that we have is a trust from God, and we must give back the first-fruits of our labor and our success. Money alone is not enough; we must also care for others in need and remember Jesus words in Matthew 25:31-46: "Inasmuch as ye have done it unto one of the least of these my brethren, ye have done it unto me."

110

We know that Christ is raised and dies no more
John B. Geyer, b. 1932
Source: *Hymns and Songs,* 1969

Of the hymn based on Romans 6 the author has written, " 'We know that Christ was raised' was written in 1967, when I was tutor at Cheshunt College, Cambridge, U.K. At that time a good deal of work was going on round the corner (involving a number of American research students) producing living cells ('the baby in the test tube'). The hymn attempted to illustrate the Christian doctrine of baptism in relation to those experiments. Originally intended as a hymn for the Sacrament of Baptism, it has become popular as an Easter hymn."

We plow the fields, and scatter
Matthias Claudius, 1740-1815
Trans. Jane M. Campbell, 1817-1878
Source: *Garland of Song,* 1861

Claudius was a commissioner of agriculture in Germany, and his poem, *Paul Eardmann's Festival* (1782), gives a romantic picture of the celebration of harvest in a German farmhouse. Its theses is that we must cooperate with God by ploughing and sowing, but God provides wind, sunshine and rain to bring forth the fruits. The hymn is an expression of humble and thankful hearts for all of God's good gifts around us.

We praise Thee, O God, our Redeemer, Creator
Julia Bulkley Cady Cory, 1882-1963
Source: *Hymns of the Living Church,* 1910

Because the older familiar hymn, "We gather together to ask the Lord's blessings", was too "Old Testament" in its concepts, Mrs. Cory at the suggestion of J. Archer Gibson, organist at Birch Presbyterian Church in New City, wrote an entirely new text for the Dutch tune KREMSER and it was first sung there on Thanksgiving day in 1902.

We three kings of Orient are
John Henry Hopkins, 1820-1891
Source: *Carols, Hymns and Songs,* 1863

After a career as a reporter and tutor, Hopkins became an Episcopal minister with interests in music. His Epiphany hymn is based on the visit of the Wise Men (Matthew 2:1-11) and is the first modern American Christmas carol. The hymn with its dialogue style with each of the Wise Men singing a stanza has become an American classic in Christmas dramas.

We would see Jesus: Lo, His star is shining
John Edgar Park, 1879-1956
Source: *Worship and Song,* 1913
In John 12:21 Philip said, "Sir, we would see Jesus." Park, who had recently written two books on the Sermon on the Mount wrote the hymn "for youth and promise and sunshine. . .and an inner glimpse of the Young Man of Nazareth living and moving among us." The various stanzas are based on events in the life of Christ.

Welcome, happy morning
Venantius Fortunatus, 535-609
Trans. John Ellerton, 1826-1893
Source: *Tempore Florigero* (In Springtime), c. 582
The 110 lines on the Resurrection by the Bishop of Poitiers have been the source for several translations, the other most famous being "Hail thee, festival day." The hymn portrays the coming of spring as a symbol of the new life which sprang forth in the world with Christ's rising from the tomb and as the tribute of nature to the triumphant Lord.

Were you there when they crucified my Lord?
Negro Spiritual
In *The Companion to the Hymnal* (Methodist) (1970) Dr. Fred Gealy wrote, "The poignancy of this spiritual is most deeply felt when one remembers that the Negro, having seen lynched bodies on the 'tree,' easily identified himself with his crucified Lord. The spirituals generally interpret the biblical stories rather than recount them. The singer stands in the midst of the event and. . .finds himself at the foot of the cross."

What a friend we have in Jesus
Joseph Medlicott Scriven, 1819-1886
Source: *Social Poems, Original and Selected,* 1865
The Canadian author (Port Hope, Ontario) wrote the hymn to comfort his mother in a time of deep sorrow but did not admit his authorship until near the end of his life. It is obviously not great poetry, but it is equally obvious that it was born of deep experience and expresses a sentiment which has comforted millions of singers.

What Child is this
William Chatterton Dix, 1837-1898
Source: *Christmas Carols New and Old,* 1871
The three stanzas are taken from a longer poem, "The Manger Throne", written c. 1865 on Epiphany Day, after the author had

read the Gospel for the day, Matthew 2:1-12. The tune GREEN-SLEEVES was already popular in 1580 when a license was granted to two different men on the same day for songs about *Lady Greene Sleeves.* Twelve days later it appeared with a sacred text and has been a popular carol tune ever since.

What God ordains is always good
(Whatever God ordains is right)
Samuel Rodigast, 1649-1708
Trans. Catherine Winkworth, 1827-1878
Source: Appendix to *Das Hannoverische Gesangbuch,* 1676

Based on Deuteronomy 32:4 ("He is the Rock, his work is perfect: for all his ways are judgment: a God of truth and without iniquity, just and right is he") the hymn has the same opening line as an older hymn by Johann Altenburg. They were written to comfort and cheer a close friend, Severus Gastorius (cantor of one of Jena's Lutheran churches). It is a superb hymn of trust in God in every situation.

What star is this that beams so bright
Charles Coffin, 1676-1749
Trans. John Chandler, 1806-1876
Source: *Paris Breviary,* 1736

"There shall come a Star out of Jacob" (Numbers 24:17) is the basis for this hymn by Coffin, the chief hymnographer of the Roman Catholic 18th century liturgical revival. A star led the Wise Men to Bethlehem, and it is Christ the Star who is the guide for our lives.

What wondrous love is this
American Folk Hymn
Source: *Southern Harmony,* 1835

The melody for this hymn shows signs of Celtic influences, and the unusual meter is that of an old sea chanty about Captain Kidd. The tune first appeared in the valleys of the Southern Appalachians, where William Walker recorded it and included it in his historic *Southern Harmony.* Each stanza has a single thought which is underscored by repetition, but it is the haunting melody which has made this hymn so popular in this country.

When all Thy mercies, O my God
Joseph Addison, 1672-1719
Source: *Spectator,* August 9, 1712

After an essay about Gratitude, in which Addison (brilliant English politician and editor) wrote, "if gratitude is due from man to man, how much more from man to his Maker! Every blessing we enjoy, by what means soever it may be derived from us, is the gift of him who is the great Author of good and Father of mercies.'' He concluded with this hymn. Its 13 stanzas express thanks to God for the whole of life — conception, birth, childhood, old age, and death.

When I survey the wondrous cross
Isaac Watts, 1674-1748
Source: *Hymns and Spiritual Songs,* 1707
More than one hymnologist has called this the finest hymn in the English language. It was included in Watts' hymns ''for the Holy Ordinance of the Lord's Supper,'' but its theme is larger than the sacrament. Our gaze is fixed entirely on the cross, but stanza two (based on Galatians 6:14) warns us not to glory in ourselves. In stanza three we see the unveiling of the heart of God, filled with sorrow and love for us. A fourth stanza, unfortunately usually omitted, is startling: ''His dying crimson like a robe.'' When we feel something of the horror of the crucifixion we are confronted with the demand of the cross: ''my soul, my life, my all.''

When in our music God is glorified
Fred Pratt Green, b. 1903
Source: *The Hymn,* July 1973
This hymn was written by the retired Methodist minister-hymnist for a Festival of Praise in 1972 to be sung to Stanford's tune ENGELBERG. No finer hymn has been written about the reasons for the use of music in worship, and it is reassuring to know that a new hymn can become immensely popular world-wide in a few short years while the author is still living. No hymnal editor would dare omit this hymn.

When morning gilds the skies
Anon. Germany, 19th Century. Trans. Edward Caswall,
    1814-1878 and Robert S. Bridges, 1844-1920
Source: *Katholisches Gesangbuch,* 1828
The focus of this hymn is praise to Jesus Christ, and it is essentially a hymn of praise — not a morning hymn. Any time is the right time to praise Christ — morning, evening, work, or prayer. The original text had 14 stanzas, and hymnal editors make different choices, which creates slightly different versions in various hymnals. Barnby's tune, written for this text, has helped to make the hymn popular with its final rousing phrase for ''May Jesus Christ be praised.''

When Stephen, full of power and grace
Jan Struther, 1901-1953

Source: *Songs of Praise,* 1931

Joyce Placzek (nee Anstruther), who used the pseudonym Jan Struther, contributed 12 new hymns to the historic British *Songs of Praise.* This hymn was specifically requested to fill a need for hymns about St. Stephen, the first Christian martyr. Her text is based on Acts, chapters 6 and 7, and tells the story almost in carol style. In America it is often sung to the early folk tune SALVATION from the 1815 *Kentucky Harmony.*

Where charity and love prevail
Latin Antiphon, Carolingian era, 9th Century
Trans. Omer Westendorf, b. 1916
Source: *People's Mass Book,* 1961

This is a hymn about the love which Christ showed for us, and the love which we are expected to show to each other. In the pre-Vatican II rite it is the last and indispensable song to be sung during the washing of feet in the Maundy Thursday communion service. The translator is a native of Cincinnati who has composed over 35 hymns and has compiled four Catholic hymnals, culminating in the *People's Mass Book.*

Where cross the crowded ways of life
Frank Mason North, 1850-1935
Source: *Christian City,* June 1903

This is probably the earliest Christian hymn of the modern city. North, a Methodist Missionary Society secretary and editor of *Christian City,* wrote the hymn looking down on the busy canyons of New York City. Based on Matthew 22:9 ("Go ye therefore unto the partings of the highways") it is a poignant picture of Christ's concerns for the down-trodden and needy people of every city.

While shepherds watched their flocks by night
Nahum Tate, 1652-1715
Source: *The Supplement to the New Version of Psalms by Dr. Brady and Mr. Tate,* 1700

The Supplement contained 16 hymns to be added to the *New Version* psalter (1696) including this paraphrase of the nativity story in Luke 2:8-14. Unlike many settings of the period, Tate's version turns prose into poetry while keeping close to the text of scripture. The lines are understandable and singable, and the finished product a shining jewel.

Ye holy angels bright
John Hampden Gurney, 1802-1862

Source: *Psalms and Hymns,* 1838

Richard Baxter (1615-1691), an English clergyman who "grew too Puritan for bishops and too Episcopalian for the Presbyterians," wrote a hymn beginning with this first line. Gurney selected stanzas and ideas and created a new hymn which is not about angels but rather a call to praise God. Angels, the departed souls in heaven, the church on earth, and any singer of the hymn ("My soul, bear thou thy part") all share in the endless praise of God.

Ye servants of God, your Master proclaim
Charles Wesley, 1707-1788
Source: *Hymns for Times of Trouble and Persecution,* 1744

Four hymns from the collection had the strange title, "Hymns to be sung in a Tumult" and refer to the absurd and slanderous accusation that the Wesleys were attempting to overthrow the Crown. Their meetings were broken up, their people mobbed, plundered, and dragged before magistrates. As Frank Colquhoun has written, "We can readily picture the small but heroic Methodist bands facing the fury of their enemies with a triumphant song like this upon their lips." The hymn is now a hymn of praise extolling God's sovereignty and magnifying the glories of Christ.

Ye watchers and ye holy ones
Athelstan Riley, 1858-1945
Source: *The English Hymnal,* 1906

Riley, who helped edit *The English Hymnal* (1906) and translated Latin and Greek hymns, wrote this festive hymn for the tune LASST UNS ERFREUEN (Let us rejoice). The first stanza names the nine orders of angels who praise God. The "bearer of the eternal Word" in stanza 2 is the Virgin Mary. Stanza three adds in all the "souls in endless rest" who have arrived in heaven, and finally we are urged to join our voices in "supernal anthems" to the Holy Trinity. No one is exempt from singing!

You satisfy the hungry heart
(See: Gift of Finest Wheat)

117

A BRIEF SELECTED BIBLIOGRAPHY

A Dictionary of Hymnology. John Julian, ed. Reprint of 1907 edition. Dover Publications, 1957.

A Hundred Years of Hymns Ancient and Modern. W. K. Lowther-Clarke. Clowes, 1960.

A Hymn Companion. Frank Colquhoun. Hodder and Stoughton, 1985.

A Panorama of Christian Hymnody. Erik Routley. GIA, 1979.

A Short Bibliography for the Study of Hymns. James R. Sydnor, ed. Hymn Society of America, Paper XXV, 1964.

A Short Companion to "Hymns and Songs" (A Supplement to The Methodist Hymn Book). John Wilson. Methodist Church Music Society, Novello, 1969.

A Survey of Christian Hymnody. William J. Reynolds. Holt Rinehart Winston, Inc. 1963.

American Negro Songs and Spirituals. John W. Work. Bonanza Books, 1940.

An English-Speaking Hymnal Guide. Erik Routley. GIA, 1979.

Catherine Winkworth. Robin A. Leaver. Concordia Publishing House, 1978.

Christian Hymns. Luther Noss, ed. World Publishing, 1963.

Companion to Congregational Praise. K. L. Parry and Erik Routley. Independent Press, Ltd., 1953.

Companion to Hymnbook for Christian Worship. Arthur N. Wake. The Bethany Press, 1970.

Companion to the School Hymn-Book of the Methodist Church. William S. Kelynack, Epworth Press, 1950.

Companion to the Service Book and Hymnal. William A. Seaman. The Commission on the Liturgy and Hymnal, 1976.

Companion to Westminster Praise. Erik Routley. Hinshaw Music, 1977.

Crusade Hymn Stories. Cliff Barrows. Hope Publishing Co., 1967.

Die Melodien der deutschen evangelischen Kirchenlieder. Johannes Zahn. Hildesheim: G. Olms (1893). 1963 reprint.

Faith Looking Forward. Brian Wren and Peter Cutts. Hope Publishing Co. , 1983.

Forty True Stories of Famous Gospel Songs. Ernest K. Emurian. W. A. Wilde Co., 1959.

Four Centuries of Scottish Psalmody. Millar Patrick. Oxford University Press, 1949.

Great Hymns and Their Stories. W. J. Limmer Sheppard. Lutterworth Press, 1950.

Guide to the Pilgrim Hymnal. Albert C. Ronander and Ethel K. Porter. United Church Press, 1966.

Handbook for American Catholic Hymnals. J. Vincent Higginson. Hymn Society of America, 1976.

Handbook on Brethren Hymns. Ruth B. Statler and Nevin W. Fisher. The Brethren Press, 1959.

Handbook to the Church Hymnary with Supplement. James Moffatt and Millar Patrick. Oxford University Press, 1927.

Handbook to the Hymnal. William C. Covert and Calvin W. Laufer. Presbyterian Board of Christian Education, 1935.

Handbook to the Mennonite Hymnary. Lester Hostetler. General Conference of the Mennonite Church of North America Board of Publications, 1949.

Historical Companion to Hymns Ancient and Modern. Maurice Frost. William Clowes & Sons, Ltd., 1962.

History of American Catholic Hymnals. J. Vincent Higginson. Hymn Society of America, 1982.

Hymn Lore. Calvin W. Laufer. Westminster Press, 1932.

Hymn Tune Names, Their Sources and Significance. Robert G. McCutchan. Abingdon Press, 1957.

Hymn Tunes and Their Story. James T. Lightwood. The Epworth Press, 1935.

Hymnal Companion to the Lutheran Book of Worship. Marilyn Stulken. Fortress Press, 1981.

Hymnal for Colleges and Schools. E. Harold Geer, ed. Yale University Press, 1956.

Hymnal Handbook for Standard Hymns and Gospel Songs. Homer A. Rodeheaver. Rodeheaver Co., 1931. Reprint AMS Press, 1970.

Hymnody Past and Present. C. S. Phillips. SPCK, 1937.

Hymns and Human Life. Erik Routley. John Murray, 1952 (rev. 1958).

Hymns and Tunes Indexed. David W. Perry. The Hymn Society of Great Britain and Ireland, and the Royal School of Church Music, 1980.

Hymns: How to Sing Them. Mandus A. Egge and Janet Moede. Augsburg Publishing House, 1966.

Hymns of Our Faith, A Handbook for the Baptist Hymnal. William J. Reynolds. Broadman Press, 1964.

Hymns of the Church, A Companion to The Hymnary of The United Church of Canada. Alexander Macmillan. The United Church Publishing House, 1935.

Hymns Today and Tomorrow. Erik Routley. Abingdon Press, 1964.

Hymns Unbidden. M. W. England and M. Sparrow. New York Public Library, 1966.

Hymns We Love. Cecil Northcott. The Westminister Press, 1954.

If Such Holy Song. The Story of the Hymns in The Hymn Book (Canada) 1971. Stanley L. Osborne. The Institute of Church Music, Whitby, Ontario, 1976.

I'll Praise My Maker. Erik Routley. Independent Press, 1951.

Lift Every Heart. Collected Hymns. Timothy Dudley Smith. Hope Publishing Co., 1984.

Living Stories of Famous Hymns. Ernest K. Emurian. W. A. Wilde Co., 1955.

Lyric Religion: The Romance of Immortal Hymns. H. Augustine Smith. D. Appleton-Century Company, 1931.

Modern Gospel Songs Stories. Haldor Lillenas. Lillenas Publishing Co., 1952.

One by One. . . .Cyril Taylor turns the pages of "100 Hymns for Today." Royal School of Church Music, 1970.

Our Hymnody: A Manual of The Methodist Hymnal, 2nd ed. Robert G. McCutchan. Abingdon Press, 1942.

Popular Hymns and Their Writers. Norman Mable. Independent Press, 1946-1951.

Praising a Mystery. Brian Wren. Hope Publishing Co., 1986.

Sing with Understanding. James P. Davies. Covenant Press, 1966.

Songs of Praise Discussed. Percy Dearmer and Archibald Jacob. Oxford University Press, 1933.

Story of the American Hymn. Edward S. Ninde. Abingdon Press, 1921. Reprinted AMS Press Inc., 1975.

Sursum Corda. S. H. Moore. Independent Press, 1956.

The Baptist Hymn Book Companion. Hugh Martin, ed. Psalms and Hymns Trust, 1962.

The English Hymn. Louis F. Benson. John Knox reprint of 1915 edition.

The Gospel in Hymns. Albert E. Bailey. Charles Scribner's Sons, 1950.

The Handbook to the Lutheran Hymnal. William G. Polack. Concordia Publishing House, 1958.

The Harvard University Hymn Book. Harvard University Press, 1964.

The Hymnal 1940 Companion. Arthur Farlander and Leonard Elinwood. The Church Pension Fund, 1949.

The Hymns and Ballads of Fred Pratt Green. Hope Publishing Co., 1982.

The Methodist Hymn-Book Illustrated in History and Experience. John Telford. The Epworth Press, 1934.

The Music of Christian Hymnody. Erik Routley. Independent Press, 1957

The Music of Christian Hymns. Erik Routley. GIA, 1981.

The Music of the Methodist Hymn-Book. James T. Lightwood, ed. and rev. by Francis B. Westbrook. The Epworth Press, 1955.

The Singers and Their Songs. Charles H. Gabriel. The Rodeheaver Co., 1915.

The Story of Christian Hymnody. Ernest E. Ryden. Augustana Press, 1959.

The Story of Our Hymns. Armin Haeussler. Eden Publishing House, 1952.

The Story of the Church's Song. Millar Patrick, rev. J. R. Sydnor. John Knox Press, 1962.

Three Centuries of American Hymnody. H. W. Foote, Harvard University Press, 1940.

Twice-Born Hymns. J. Irving Erickson. Covenant Press, 1976.

Unitarian Hymn Writers. H. W. Stephenson. Lindsey Press, 1931.

Who's Who of Hymn Writers. Ronald W. Thompson. Epworth Press, 1967.